Over My Head

By Debi Wagner

An activist group fights an airport expansion:
A personal story of community, grassroots, toxic
emissions and far too many cancer deaths.

Trafford rev. 01/06/2011

 www.trafford.com

North America & international
toll-free: 1 888 232 4444 (USA & Canada)
phone: 250 383 6864 ♦ fax: 812 355 4082

This book is dedicated to the greatest activist on Earth, Minnie Brasher who reshaped my thinking, to the late Pat Pompeo who reshaped my life and Dave who filled my lonely heart with happiness.

Over My Head

By Debi Wagner

INTRODUCTION

It is my concern for people and especially helpless victims that compels me to write this book. So many people are affected by this problem without knowing the serious nature and effects of what they are exposed to that also makes me want to share my knowledge and experience to inform and warn of the risks. I have been trying for decades to force agencies and the industry to get more involved to protect and inform the public. I have not been as successful as I would have hoped for maybe two reasons; the costs to the industry would be enormous so any inroad to change is vigorously opposed; and the information is so obscure, vague, contradictory and difficult to understand that it needs a full time vocation for any individual or group to make a case. So it is my hope, in writing this book, that the public will become informed and this will push the industry to take responsibility for its actions and provide meaningful solutions.

There has been a lot of attention focused on the problem of jet aviation noise. Homes have been insulated, some have been bought out, new standards have quieted jet engines, but there has been very little attention and work done on what I believe to be a much more serious problem of jet aviation emissions. The fact that there are so many commercial airports located in largely populated areas in this country makes me worry constantly about the extent of the harm falling on and infiltrating this population. Especially in light of a 1970 report by the Department of Commerce showing the impacted area by jet aircraft emissions starting at the runway ends and extending 12 miles outward in a fan shaped area 12 miles wide, making the entire effected area over 25 miles in diameter surrounding the airport of study, Seattle-Tacoma International (Sea-Tac).[1] Regulators would argue with me that this study is too old and therefore, useless. I counter with the fact it is the only one of its kind I am aware of and there has been nothing credible debating the conclusions. To the contrary, some of the suggestions for emissions reduction posed in 1973 are still on the table in 2010 awaiting implementation, carried over into more current recommendations even though nobody will acknowledge the 1973 reports dire warnings of eminent danger to the exposed public due to its age. Too old, too antiquated, doesn't apply when it is still relevant today because nothing has changed except there are more operations making the problems worse.

Predating the introduction of jets into commercial service, the area known as Highline located closest to Sea-Tac, well within the 25 mile boundary, was the most populated by acre of any other in the state of Washington. The local school district had more children enrolled than any other in the state. Many of the schools pre-date the airport and one even pre-dates the invention of flying. When discussing the noise effect from jets on local populations I have often heard the media and agencies say that these people knew there was an airport there before they moved in so they knew what they were getting, property was cheaper so they get what they deserve. This argument is cruel abuse for those who were there before regular jet service became the standard and is insidious if the industry knew so many might be harmed by emissions that agencies and airport sponsors, knowing the risks, neither warned of or acknowledged as a problem.

Although I have concluded the industry has been silent or in denial regarding this issue, they would likely counter they have put the information out there for public view. This is true in a sense since most of the information I have comes directly from the industry. However, some of the quotes from Sea-Tac owner and operator, Port of Seattle, are so confusing, it is a full time job for somebody to untangle what they are saying, which I made my pastime for about 10 years. As an outgrowth of my pastime, I spent countless hours researching any airport emission study I could find and enlisted the help of some local air pollution engineers to help me understand what I was reading. I co-founded a national aviation watch association, was twice elected president of the local grassroots organization fighting airport expansion and sat as administrative director of an umbrella organization, a politically funded group. I am considered an aviation emission expert by many professionals across the country, just for the mere fact that I am the only activist that has studied this issue. But in reality, I was just a mom who was concerned about my family.

What I discovered in my research was mind boggling. I found that jets produce dozens of dangerous emissions. Cancer causing chemicals from fueling and engine use are combined together in a toxic stew that rivals and even exceeds the worst industrial pollution sources such as incinerators and refineries for volume and surpasses them in risk factors. What is more alarming is there are hundreds of thousands, maybe millions of people living close to many of the nation's airports who are completely unaware of the terrible risk they are being exposed to 24 hours a day. Worse yet, the industry knows this but hides behind the ambiguity of emission identification, the amount of time it takes for cancer to show up in an individual, the lack of regulation of airports as sources of toxic emissions and the downright denial produced in industry reports.

Now consider there is more automobile, truck and bus traffic around airports added to the mix of an already over saturated pollution load from the jets and you have a giant, unregulated, unmonitored, exempt, dangerous polluter nobody understands and most regulators are ignoring. To cite just three examples of the volume of emissions, in a 20 year period, while all industry and cars increased their pollution levels by 3% or less of given pollutants, aviation increased theirs by 133% (ozone precursors, volatile organic compounds [VOC] and nitrogen oxides)[2]. In a recent greenhouse gas inventory report compiled for the State of Washington, nearly ¼ of the King County total was attributable to Sea-Tac Airport jets which, in my opinion, makes Sea-Tac, as a facility, the single largest producer of greenhouse gas emissions in the state.[3] One 2 minute DC-10 takeoff produces an amount of emissions equal to 21,530 cars for nitrogen oxides and VOC's and according to a physicist who calculated emission facts to verify my findings, sulfur oxides equaling nearly a half million cars for one 747 10 minute idle.[4] Pumping nearly 2 million gallons of Jet A fuel each day is a huge amount with its accompanying atmospheric effects when burnt, most of which is released into the upper atmosphere over our heads where, to my knowledge, apart from global warming, long term effects on the planet have not yet been seriously studied.

While I was on my quest for emission information, Sea-Tac was getting ready to launch its Environmental Impact Statement (EIS) for a third runway, meaning more of what I considered to be too much already. As I dug further into the Port and its practices through the EIS process, I became more knowledgeable about airport noise and water problems as well. As these are also very serious issues, I can't say enough for all the tireless efforts of many activists in the various groups I have encountered. I also learned that our battles are not unique. These same battles are being played out again and again all over the world as airports expand and grow.

In 1994, our local grassroots group had nearly 3,000 members, the umbrella organization had funding, a web site, newsletter and staff and our local cities had collected several million dollars to launch a legal challenge to airport expansion plans. Our respective group membership included former FAA employees, Boeing engineers, a physicist, doctors, lawyers, politicians, economists, former EPA regulators, water quality experts and a whole bunch of really nice people. We had probably the most sophisticated battle plan ever launched against an airport expansion by an angry bunch of citizens

I've ever heard of. With millions of dollars collected to fund a legal challenge to the runway and one of the most knowledgeable legal teams on airport expansion projects in the country, it seemed nearly impossible to me that this runway plan could ever succeed.

I have recently been reading "The Sydney Airport Fiasco" by Paul Fitzgerald. He tells the political, social and environmental story behind what went into the planning, building and commission of the third runway at Kingsford-Smith Airport (KSA) in Australia. His book is well written, organized and informative. The differences between his book and mine are a few names, places and his is more of a political look into the deceptions that went on while mine is more of a personal one. The events leading up to the third runway at KSA and what happened after it opened are so similar to the events at Sea-Tac I could have re-titled his book the Sea-Tac Airport Fiasco, changed a few names and hardly anyone could tell the difference.

It makes me believe that the development of airport expansion plans and building of runways are all taught at the same school, maybe called; "How to wreck havoc with the public and not let them know what is happening to them until it is too late", school for consultants, compromised judges, political climbers, plants and gutless agencies.

At any time during the planning process of EIS's for the third Sea-Tac runway, I could have turned to any given page of the thousands of pages of narrative and data, and pointed out a law about to be broken. It didn't matter for us and as far as I can tell, it hasn't made a difference in other similar battles either.

Since this was mainly an environmental battle over excessive noise, air and water pollution tied to a single industry, I would have thought that a host of environmental groups would have become involved. They haven't. Sierra Club, Friends of the Earth and the Puget Sound Keepers have been slightly but never seriously involved throughout the last two decades. Waste Action Project, a small environmental group, mainly involved with water quality issues, is the only one who has been regularly attentive to the airport pollution problems.

Maybe more haven't become involved because they believe the problems are isolated near the facility. But with atmospheric pollution deposited all over the county from above, and wastewater entering the Pacific Ocean it isn't really isolated to just the Highline area.

Contaminated wastewater from airport sources flows down three creeks and empties into the Puget Sound. Members of our group have videoed the suffering and dying of salmon trying to breathe in these creeks as they return to spawn. Yet no large, well funded environmental organization has stepped up to the plate to champion this cause.

If my neighbor were playing the stereo at a fraction of the level of airport noise, the police could be summoned to issue a violation of the noise ordinance. But with an airport, normal environmental protection from excessive noise is exempted. I've been told; "it's an airport." I have no idea why anyone would think that would suffice, especially to someone whose life is being ruined. Would it work to say to someone who has been chemically poisoned by water leaking from a toxic waste site to say; "well it's a toxic waste site!" "What did you expect?" While everyone knows you shouldn't live near a toxic waste site, nearly nobody knows, except for the noise annoyance, that you shouldn't live within twelve miles of a runway end because of emissions. Millions of Americans made to suffer for commerce and travel just isn't reasonable if people have to give up their lives and health.

Normal environmental protection from massive amounts of toxic and cancer causing emissions doesn't apply to an airport either. They are exempted from the normal rules that apply to all industry and cars. If the airport were a smokestack it would be shut down immediately by the local air pollution control agency. Unlike a smokestack which blows emissions upward, the jet engines thrust their dangerous chemicals at full power into neighborhoods, schools, nursing homes, all sorts of sensitive land uses. Noise laws don't apply because FAA writes their own rules and sets the standards they follow and is also the enforcement agency for violation...what has been commonly termed "the fox guarding the hen house." If those standards are exceeded, they can merely write new rules and ignore the violation. Water quality standards can be set aside. Permits to pollute are issued and fuel spills, glycol in the streams, dangerous chemicals in the ground all get a slap on the wrist. This industry has so much money, they can easily pay their way through the mire of waste they create. While all other industry is required to cut its pollution levels, the aviation industry continues to increase theirs. Is anybody doing anything? Not really.

The airport has done a good job selling their programs as though they were an overly generous social service agency providing relief to thousands by insulating homes, phasing out noisier jets and cutting pollution levels. They have converted some taxis to compressed natural gas and are being recognized for their great achievements in this area. Sea-Tac has boasted they are a national leader and trendsetter in the money they have spent and the number of homes they have insulated despite the fact that an expert noise panel hired by the State of Washington in 1996 found their noise mitigation programs hadn't provided meaningful relief. Since nobody has really acknowledged Sea-Tac as the biggest noise and air polluter in the state, anything they do looks great.

The Airport Safety and Noise Abatement Act (ASNA) was written and passed into federal law in 1979. The intention of ASNA was to identify non-compatible land uses around airports and to mitigate by converting non-compatible like homes and schools, into compatible, buy-out and redevelop as open space, parking lots, etc.

An occasional jet flying over homes during the day and very few if any flying in the middle of the night, didn't cause the serious backlash that came when operations doubled in the 80's and tripled in the 90's and loads of heavy laden cargo planes found it best to take off at 3:30 a.m. Practically overnight, people were thrust into living in a war zone and with little warning if any, were left to suffer alone and forgotten with limited ability to fight and practically no way out without losing their shirt. Meanwhile, near Sea-Tac, a cheaper way to deal with the noise problem than buying out billions of dollars worth of homes was being crafted. Elsewhere, laws were being passed to give the industry vast amounts of power and clout while other laws were passed to take away the rights of individuals to have a venue for recompense. While the airport continues to assert everything is improving, knowing this is the opposite of the truth, many residents, somehow convinced they don't deserve any better treatment and worn out from fighting, either move away or give up.

I stayed and fought, at least for awhile. This is my story.

Chapter 1

HOW IT STARTED

I was lying on the couch in my living room when I heard the strangest noise. I couldn't figure out what it was. It was a sound of an engine powering up and down. Powering up was a loud high-pitched whining noise. Powering down became almost inaudible. I sat up. It was 7:30 in the morning. My children were asleep and I would soon be getting them up for school. But what was this ungodly noise. It seemed to be getting closer.

As I realized it was an airplane flying over my house, I began to panic. I have heard planes before, but this was something different. What kind of plane powers up and down like that unless it is in trouble? I jumped off the couch. It was getting louder still. I didn't want to go outside and look to see what it was because the sight of something coming straight into my house would give me a heart attack. Besides, I was in my pajamas. Do I hide? Do I run? I know I can't escape. How can I save my children from this certain doom? They are all innocently sleeping in their beds with no idea of what is happening. Power up, power down, up, down, screaming noise now, what in the world? It finally passed. My heart is pounding so hard I thought it was going to bounce its way right out of my chest. I am running back and forth through my house like a complete idiot. Nothing happened. I should be relieved. But I am not.

Just a few months before I had become eligible for the noise insulation program the airport offered but I had problems with the wording of an easement the Port wanted so I had passed on the program. Now I wondered if I had made a mistake and if something new was happening.

This experience made me start to seriously think about my situation. I am living in the flight path of a major international airport. This wasn't the case when I moved into my brand new home in 1980. It was a four bedroom on a cul-de-sac in a neighborhood of brand new homes. An elementary school was less than a block away. The neighbors were friendly. We had beautiful yards we all planted together. A few planes passed once and awhile. But as time went on the airport got busier. In 1990, without my knowledge, my beautiful little neighborhood had been designated a straight out flight path, a jet highway.

I went to the store later this same day that I heard that horrible noise and I asked people if they had heard it. Several people said they had and wondered what it was.

I decided to call the airport and I asked them what had happened. They actually used to answer the phone back in 1994 when people called the noise complaint hot-line. Years later, it would be a long recorded message that asked 10 questions about who you are, speak slowly, spell your name, where you live, what you heard, when it happened, type of plane, airline if known, direction of flight, wind speed, temperature, longitude, (just kidding) and where they could reach you should they decide to respond. In my experience, by the time I am done with this questionnaire, my anger has shifted from the airplane noise to the message line. They need another line for complaints about the message line. The staff this day however, confirmed that a military plane, one of those giant transport jets, had landed that morning at Sea-Tac Airport. I asked how that can happen since it is a civilian airport. They said that Sea-Tac is allowed to take them if they cannot land at the military base and because

McChord Air Force Base to the south had been socked in with fog, Sea-Tac was the next closest airfield for diversion in this emergency. This was not comforting news to me.

This single event was going to change my life completely. I was going to become embroiled in one of the most difficult and longest battles of my life. I was going to give up nearly everything I owned and I was going to meet some of the nicest people, wonderful, innocent, dedicated sheep for the slaughter.

About a week later I was reading the local newspaper and noticed a community calendar bulletin for a meeting of an anti-noise group at the local Highline School District headquarters. I decided to attend.

I really don't remember much of what they said at the meeting, but learned the four cities closest to the airport had formed what was called the Airport Communities Coalition (ACC) and were planning to sue the Port of Seattle (Port, owner and operator of Sea-Tac) if they tried to build a third runway. Another group, the Regional Commission on Airport Affairs, (RCAA) was running a web site and sending out a quarterly newsletter. They considered themselves an umbrella organization leading the many groups that had sprung up to fight airport noise and expansion. The host of the meeting, Citizens Against Sea-Tac Expansion (CASE), a grassroots citizens group, had nearly 3,000 members with about 100 attending each monthly meeting like this one. I noticed most of the people at the meeting were elderly. I sat by a nice younger lady, Tanya who was presently the secretary for CASE. She gave me her phone number.

After about a week, I was working in my yard when I noticed the planes going over. I hadn't paid any attention to them before, but now, I noticed every single one. I realized I was listening to the engines and each type of plane had a distinctive sound. DC-10's had a whine, a 727 sounded like a repeating backfire, 747's had a low droning rumble. It seemed like they were going over my house constantly. I couldn't figure out why I hadn't noticed them before. But it started to make me wonder what would happen if one just dropped out of the sky. Would it plow a hole through the earth for blocks or would it drop straight down and make a giant crater? Would it fall onto my house or veer off into the Puget Sound? What were the odds? There didn't seem to be very many crashes so I guess I was pretty safe. I could just sit in my house and wait and listen. I could twiddle my thumbs until something didn't sound right again and then I could run around like a nut until I realized I had nowhere to go.

I called Tonya. We talked for awhile. I could hear something in the background and she told me it was engine run-ups at the airport. She said she lived to the west of the airport and when the wind was just right, the noise from the run-ups was horrendous. I didn't know what run-ups were so she explained to me that when the jet engines are serviced, they run them at full power for a minute or so and then wind them down. You can tell the difference between run-ups and takeoffs because run-ups don't fade away, they suddenly stop. I couldn't hear it from my house because I was two miles to the south, not near enough to the runways to hear the ground noise. Tonya asked me to wait a minute each time it rose to full power making it very difficult to have our conversation. I felt some relief that at least I didn't have to put up with that. As we talked, Tonya decided I should call someone else, someone she said was the best expert on all the airport issues in the area. She gave me Minnie's phone number.

Chapter 2

THEY WANT WHAT?

My turn for the Airport's insulation program had come up about a year after I applied. My neighbors had been insulated and called me over to see their new windows. They had been impressed with the work and thought I might want to get it, since according to their estimation, it was free. Prior to being scared out of my wits by the military plane, I had thought it might be a good thing to do as it appeared on the surface, to have improved my neighbors' house and they perceived the noise from overhead jets had been somewhat reduced.

I had to attend insulation school so they could confuse me with their DNL, (day-night noise level) decibel event and average lingo. The noise remedy office was located in Maywood Elementary, one of the Highline Schools that was considered too noisy, closed to students and subsequently absorbed by the airport. I noticed they had air conditioners in every window. I thought this was interesting since at the time, none of the Highline schools had air conditioners so these would have been installed by the Port of Seattle for their noise remedy staff.

According to the noise map prominently displayed on the wall in the entryway, my home appeared to be in the 75 DNL zone.

Negative health and property value effects were expected if living with levels 65 DNL and above. According to the Environmental Protection Agency (EPA), 45 decibels is the level at which disturbance (adverse health effects) begins. The greatest amount of interior noise level reduction that can be achieved by insulation is allegedly 20 decibels (db). The 65 DNL is a result of constant noise averaged over a year. Understanding how the Port and the Federal Aviation Administration (FAA) uses the DNL average is a complex study of its own that could probably fill another several volumes of books that I don't have the expertise for. I do know that hidden within the averages there are many spikes over 100 db, theoretically damaging to health and hidden within interpretation of the averages are many exceptions including exclusions and nullifications. For instance, an international carrier is exempt from US noise rules and may make more noise than allowed but is not counted in the total average. Planes under 75,000 pounds are not required to meet the noise standards so are excluded from the average. Unscheduled flights are exempted. Night time noise receives a 10 db penalty that can be bought down by the noise maker from a quieter airline. If a noise monitor malfunctions or produces data that is considered unusual, it will be discounted, reduced or nullified.

Insulation affixed to my home would only be expected to bring the interior noise level down to 55 DNL which was above EPA standard, but apparently, acceptable to the FAA and the Port as long as I waived my rights to ever claim damages, a caveat neatly tucked into their "Avigation Easement". They forgot to tell me this bit of information at insulation school. They also failed to mention a judge had ordered the Port to counsel me to talk to a lawyer about the easement, a "legal document," if I had any questions.

Another program the Port offered called transaction assistance, would give me the option to sell my home with the Port's help and promised to provide me with fair market value. At insulation school, they assured me I was not eligible for transaction assistance. I would find out some time later that homes in the 75 DNL are eligible, but would still have to argue my way into being acknowledged as eligible. The staff at insulation school didn't discuss details of the transaction assistance program with me but I found out how it works. The Port's contract appraiser would determine the value of a home, a homeowners real estate agent of their choosing would attempt to sell the home at that price and if not sold during this first marketing period, the Port would cash out the homeowner at the appraisers price, keep 10% for real estate fees and continue to drop the price using their own contracted real estate agent until the house sold. The buyer of any transaction assisted home would never be offered any such help or programs. The easement would stay attached to the title and any new owner would automatically be subject to the profound waivers included in that document.

Fair market value, according to George Sutter, the first manager of the Port's acquisition/relocation program, was defined as what a home would be worth if it were not in an area affected by airport noise. What most people didn't know was the appraisers were required to use homes outside the noise insulation program boundaries, but as close to the airport as possible. Since homes across the street from the noise insulation boundary are just as devalued as the homes inside the boundary, most people never received enough money to move away, but ended up back into the noise zone, just a mile or so from where they had been before. My next door neighbors were people who had been relocated from a home in the buy-out area of 85 DNL to an un-insulated home in my neighborhood in the 75 DNL. They went from super unhealthy, extremely noisy to really noisy and very unhealthy. Their previous mortgage had been almost paid off, but because the Port had given them so little for their old home, with no extra for interest rate differential, which is required in the Uniform Relocation Assistance Act, their retirement had to be pushed back another 10 years due to a higher home price, higher interest rate and longer term mortgage they could barely afford. This was even in a neighborhood that was also experiencing airport induced devaluation!

A booklet that was mailed to me prior to my attending insulation school explained some of the terms and conditions of the insulation work, easement and waivers. I still have my booklet and 17 years later, I am still wondering how a government agency could get away with this kind of thing. Not only would the Port no longer be liable for damages if they made more noise than the agreement allowed, the easement would allow access in any proximity for planes to pass over, through or in between my home. The agreement requires that homeowner:

> "…conveys and warrants to the Port, its successors and assigns, a permanent and non-exclusive easement for the free and unobstructed use and passage of all types of aircraft (as hereinafter defined) through the airspace over and in the vicinity of the Premises, with such use and passage to be unlimited as to frequency, type of aircraft, and ***proximity***."[5] (bold italics added)

As for the effects of insulation:

> "The Port does not represent or warrant that Homeowner will experience any improvement in the noise levels within the Premises as a result of any work undertaken as part of the program."[6]

As for the performance of the work:

> "Homeowner agrees that the Port…shall not be liable and further waives all claims for expenses and damages, for any injury (<u>including death</u>) to any person or for damage to any property sustained, or alleged to have been sustained, as a result of or in connection with any work undertaken as part of the Program."[7] (emphasis added) "The Port further makes no warranties and disclaims any responsibility or liability for the manner or quality of any work undertaken or materials supplied."[8]

Their workers could destroy my home, even kill me, or a plane could drive right through my house and I would have no claim for damages. Shocking and outrageous!

At a recent meeting with the airport staff, a homeowner said their windows were pulling away from the wall, were fogged from moisture inside the many panes and rot was developing around the frame. The Port told the homeowner that the company who built the windows went out of business, those types of windows were no longer made and the homeowner would have no recourse other than try to repair the damage themselves. This is no small task either. Everything is custom made. Besides the heat loss, mold from moisture, wood rot and impaired visibility out the window, the homeowner nullifies the agreement by modifying the insulation. Now the Port has an easement and waiver excusing themselves and their contractors from any liability while the homeowner is living in an unhealthy noise level in a damaged home way outside the normal realm of reasonable repair.

According to Port documents, if after insulated, I claimed that noise had not been reduced enough or got louder in the future, it would be my responsibility to pay for monitoring of the noise with the Port's equipment for an entire year, allow them to interpret the data and compare it to the rules they set. No matter how disturbed I am, as long as their paperwork shows I am O.K., there is nothing, no law, no act, no protection I could turn to for help. If they somehow miraculously admit noise is violating the rules, it would still be my responsibility to legally argue for damages. The easement cannot be nullified. The military jet that had passed over my house and initially got me into this whole mess in the first place, wouldn't even be counted in the noise measurements because it was exempted twice, first because it was military and military and foreign carriers are not included in noise data and secondly because it was not a scheduled flight.

My father had owned a title company and my mom was a real estate broker so my first instinct was to find out more about the easement and whether it would affect the value or a sale of my property. A local title company I called told me the easement would be a defect on the title and that it had value. Usually homeowners are paid money to grant easements. For instance, if my driveway is the only access road to a home behind me, I could charge that homeowner $10,000 dollars as a one-time fee to grant him an access on my driveway to his property. It would then be attached to my title with any exception I might add for future terms should his property change ownership. But the Port's response to this extremely broad language is that they cannot give something to anyone without payment, supposedly part of a State of Washington statute. But what about taking use and isn't this enough? I went to the noise abatement office and argued that the Port had already taken use and was giving insulation as a payment for that. Why would they take additional waivers on top of the noise and use? Their response was; "the program is voluntary, so don't sign up unless you want it." They weren't forcing me to waive my rights or get insulated. But I was being forced to live in the unhealthy environment THEY were creating…no, according to them I could just move. Move where, back into the zone because my property was so devalued? No matter what I came up with as a logical argument to their ruining my quality of life, they had a response. It was my choice if I wanted to be insulated. It was my choice if I wanted to move. It was my choice if I wanted to live in a cardboard box. What if the contractor ruined my home? That was also my choice. I didn't have to sign up, it's voluntary.

A letter I received back from the FAA a year later admitted the Port's easement contains language considered more broad than most so I appealed to the state for clarification. After months of waiting, the state responded that it is not within their purview to correct or dispel. It's a local issue. They reminded me the Port cannot give something without receiving something in return. I was right back at the beginning needing to start all over with the same argument

I had already made. Yes they can give insulation for free, state law allows it. Besides they already took use so insulation doesn't need further payment of waivers of property rights. Additionally, FAA pays 80% of the cost because it is a federal grant program we are all paying for already. It took months to get an answer and I was ready to give up. As I would find out years down the road, this scenario of sending helpless citizens on wild goose chases to get answers that take time and energy most working Americans can't spare, is so typical it must be scripted.

In this quagmire of never-ending circles of absolution the Port has built for themselves, victims of their operations are left completely helpless, totally at their mercy with no other authority to turn to for checks and balances on their programs. The cities have separated themselves from the activities of the Port, so has the county. The State allows Ports to operate completely independently from the department of transportation. At the federal level, the EPA doesn't get involved because the FAA makes the rules on the noise they create. EPA can only sit back, observe and hope for the best because at the federal level, one agency's rules are only as strong, not stronger than the other agency's rules.

I was not only upset about the new noise I had noticed, I was absolutely outraged about the easement language, suspected loss of property value and my inability to do anything about any of this so far. They had already scared the living daylights out of me. I was having trouble talking to my neighbors outside. I couldn't even imagine inviting people over for an outdoor barbeque because of the embarrassment. I was having trouble sleeping because I was lying awake listening to the engines roar over my house making sure that each audible boom, whine or roar sounded correct.

After I had passed on signing up for insulation I wrote a letter to the editor comparing the easement and the Port's behavior with Mr. Potter, the notorious opportunity grabber from the Jimmy Stewart movie; "It's a Wonderful Life." I titled my letter; "It's a Wonderful

Lie." I thought the Port and Mr. Potter were so much alike since they both fed off the hardships of innocent people usually crafted by their own sinister schemes, then lent a hand to help, attaching conditions to that help which advanced their own power while further crippling their victims leaving them totally at their mercy.

CHAPTER 3

MINNIE

Soon after my letter had appeared in the local paper and some CASE members had remarked about what a true analogy it was, I decided to call Minnie. We had a long talk over the phone. She invited me to her house and even though we had just met, she made me feel like I was her best friend. She had been in the fight against the airport for several years already and had formed her own group of three called Southwest King County Citizens. These three ladies were all near retirement age and probably should have been sitting around knitting and telling stories about their grandkids. Instead, they occupied themselves with going to any regional air transportation planning meeting they could find, sending out open act requests and arguing with the most influential politicians in our state on a regular basis.

Through her experiences at meetings Minnie had learned who could and could not be trusted. Of these politicians, and future politicians, some would occasionally show up to offer advice or support during the course of our airport fight, many who Minnie instantly identified as previously selling out the communities with their votes or unsupportive silence either for political gain or to disassociate themselves from the homeowners they considered less than smart. Minnie always knew where they really stood.

Minnie is from Texas and even though she was about 20 years older than me, she looked and acted much younger. She had boundless energy, a spitfire attitude and a sharp mind to dissect, understand and use most of the volumes of papers that covered her dining table. Almost any subject I wanted to talk about, she had several documents she could pull out and show me what had happened so far. I was truly amazed at this whole situation. I had never seen anything like this before.

Minnie explained to me the "four post plan" which began in late 1989, mediation and some of the history of the Port of Seattle.

The four post plan which put all jet departures into a narrow corridor, the south one passing directly over my house, was an outgrowth of an act passed by Congress in 1979 which directed the FAA to establish a process for addressing airport noise and land use compatibility around airports across the country. This act, known as the Airport Safety and Noise Abatement Act (ASNA) was likely the first piece of legislation that I am aware of to recognize and require FAA begin work on the problem with airport noise in neighborhoods in close proximity to many of the nation's airports. By 1994, FAA had a plan for the phase out of Stage I (noisiest) aircraft, and subsequently would phase out Stage II requiring airports to operate an all Stage III fleet before the turn of the century. Unknown to most people, there are still exceptions for operating Stage II aircraft.

The local airport would create maps depicting contours designating areas eligible for the Part 150 program which is the funding mechanism for federal financial involvement in noise abatement. The program Sea-Tac developed included buy-outs of incompatible land uses, insulation and transaction assistance. Most incompatible uses around Sea-Tac were single family homes. The airport could have used the highway as their corridor to the south with many businesses and traffic taking the brunt of the noise, but instead chose neighborhoods. Could it be that homes are the major development singled out for abuse because it is cheaper to insulate and litigate damages with homeowners than with banks, stores and hotels which are the majority of uses along the highway? The aircraft traffic could turn directly out over the Puget Sound affecting hundreds rather than thousands, but homeowners along the waterfront are probably more financially able to sue than middle class residents.

The four-post plan focused and concentrated the noise in the narrowest corridor possible. People across the street from the corridor would be considered undisturbed even if their perception differed from the noise map.

Prior to the four post plan, the Port had come up with a program called "Mediation" which assumes the communities closest to the airport want to remain intact. So instead of relocation, which would have cost billions if removing all the homes in the 65 DNL, the airport would satisfy homeowners desire to stay by instead providing a program of noise mitigation. This might be better understood as a government taking of property for use without compensation, (5th Amendment, Bill of Rights) unless you consider insulation as compensation enough.

How they did this was by putting together a group which included a few members of communities not affected by noise and one affected person from the community near the airport along with a few selected representatives from local political offices. The lone community representative was rumored to have been legally blind. I don't know if she was able to read the materials accompanying mediation, or whether she knew exactly what she was signing when it came time to ratify the agreement. But it was adopted and signed and now we're stuck with it. Once the groundwork was laid for special purpose districts to make decisions outside the usual vote and representative government decision making of the past, these and regional planning bodies now cite sewage treatment plants, prisons and runways, uses nobody wants near them but everyone seems to need. All they have to do is make sure they have majority votes from enough people unaffected by these decisions. Even though our process was clearly unfair from the get-go, and should have been challenged and thrown out, other cities around the country who were grappling with the same noise problems and the gigantic price tag of removing people from incompatible land praised and some even adopted aspects of our program. The busier the airport gets, the more impossible it is for homeowners to get out, something never discussed but now a reality.

At least one judge gave undue deference to the easement, but disregarded mediation in his validation of claims when 113 homeowners sued for noise damage claiming loss of value due to noise constituting use.

Prior to ASNA and as far back as 1971, groups of frustrated and angry residents were filing or threatening to file lawsuits against the Port for loss of value, use and enjoyment of their properties (diminution) as a result of noise from airport operations. Nine plaintiffs claimed diminution in one case and another 166 homeowners on another side of the airport experiencing what was termed 'noise and sickening fumes' were threatening to file a 60 million dollar lawsuit if the Port didn't buy them out. Homeowners complained their homes were not sellable because mortgages could not be insured. After two years of negotiations and studies, the FAA provided a grant for 2.6 million with matching funds from the Port to buy-out the 166 homes. The archive of articles Minnie had did not disclose the outcome for the group of nine.

As time went on, the noise map began to shrink. I am not sure if it was because of buy-outs and insulation, phase out of noisier aircraft, a combination of both, errors or wishful thinking. Nobody oversees this process besides the Port and Federal Aviation Administration (FAA). Experts have claimed that with increased operations, noise mitigation meant to quiet the noisiest jets has become ineffective. Level of noise and frequency of noise events are not too different in perception of annoyance. Having lived with both, my opinion is that the more frequent operation of quieter jets is just as disturbing as the less frequent loud event. At a recent meeting with airport consultants, they admitted the noise monitors don't measure low frequency noise. The constant low frequency rumble of the newer jets may cause health effects that are different from the loud spikes from noisier jets of the past. It may not be quieter if the frequency is changed and the noise monitors don't measure it. Recent studies in Germany have found blood pressure increases when people are exposed to aviation noise, but not when exposed to car, bus and train noise.

Besides so many problems people could point out about the overly expensive, time intensive and usual poor way the government generally runs many of their programs, the benefits of insulation has never been validated. For the most part one could safely argue government funded airport insulation programs all over the country have been a very costly invalidated human experiment. Nobody is available to fix the problems that have now arisen. Nobody is looking into the unusual practices attached to some of the Port's other programs.

One of the properties the Port bought out for the second runway at pennies on the dollar for the value it later brought was sold or leased to Boeing who built a warehouse parts center. The resident who had owned this farm at one time wanted to sue for the later realized commercial value but the land wasn't re-designated commercial until after it was bought as residential. As long as the property sat unused for a certain period of time, the law did not allow the original homeowner to make a claim. Many have thought this is an unfair and unconstitutional practice. The Port, a quasi government agency is able to purchase homes at low value, a value induced by their own operations, knowing beforehand it can be resold or reused at a much higher commercial rate. In my opinion there is little difference between knowledge of potential buyers of induced prices and insider trading. But there is no watch dog of the buy-out program and really nobody these people can go to with their complaints. The homeowner had no other option than to sell to the Port since the home was in the highest noise zone, completely uninhabitable and totally un-sellable.

Additionally, these properties in the buy-out area belong to King County taxing authority. But once sold to the Port, they are taken off the tax rolls. Essentially it costs the Port nothing to leave properties vacant and wait for the time limit to expire before commercial reuse or resale. Homeowners are left with no options. If they don't willingly sell, the Port can just take it because state law affords them the right of eminent domain.

Minnie pointed out to me that the Port has vast amounts of power and authority. According to Washington Research Council, they are, among other things, allowed to:

- "Levy property taxes, outside of the 1 percent constitutional limit.
- Sell general obligation and revenue bonds.
- Acquire land by cash, condemnation or right of eminent domain.
- Entertain for the purposes of industrial promotion or conduct any other activities, as deemed appropriate by the legislature, outside of the constitutional provision prohibiting lending the public's credit for private gain."[9]

It would appear to me this last provision exempts them from their claim they cannot gift noise mitigation without getting something in return which is why they need to extract the all inclusive easement. In essence, they have already taken use and insulation should be compensation for that alone, but why stop there when you can take more? As far back as the early 1900's when privately owned waterfront property in Seattle was taken and converted to a working water port one author had the foregoing observation:

"In the wake of a grassroots populist movement in Washington and after considerable resistance, the state legislature in 1911 passed Chapter 53.04 of the Revised Code of Washington (RCW), enabling the creation of locally controlled public port districts to promote and protect all commerce. Many private entrepreneurs considered it a radical idea bordering on socialism or communism according to Padraic Burke's book, *A History of the Port of Seattle*."[10]

The Washington Research Council also noted:

"Given their legal and taxing authorities for transportation and economic development, ports have the most flexible and far-reaching powers granted to public entities in Washington."[11]

"Taxes levied to support port operations and interest on general obligation debt, on the other hand, show up as non-operating revenues on a port's statement of revenue and expenses (essentially an income statement.)

Unlike most other units of local government, current financial reporting requirements for ports do not include a separate statement of taxes and uses as part of an annual report. In terms of property taxation, the Port of Seattle alone was the sixth largest local taxing district in Washington with its tax levy of more than $27 million in 1988."[12]

In the period 2001 to 2009 the Port's property tax collection has increased by 136% to 75.9 million.[13]

The tax levy, authorized by the legislature in 1911, gave the Port the ability to collect property tax without voter approval. Voter approved limit at .75% of the total taxable value of all property in the county in 2008 gives them the ability to obligate themselves to almost a three billion dollar debt limit. The unapproved limit at

.25% allows nearly a billion without voter approval. Nobody is in charge of how much they take, use or need except themselves. The taxing authority (usually afforded only to government agencies with representation a vote and accountability), besides insuring the Port will not go out of business also gives them the opportunity to obtain a very high bond rating. Current General Obligation Bond debt as of 12/31/2008 is $378,065,000.[14] Should all the property in the county suddenly depreciate which has recently occurred with the economic downturn, it is unclear how the Port might be forced to reduce their indebtedness, who would or could force it or what mechanism could possibly be used to accomplish this or if even anyone would care.

In 1991 KPMG Peat Marwick management consultants for Transport Canada found the Port of Seattle to be the highest tax subsidized Port on the continent.[15] Since they are one of only a few Ports on the continent who can collect property tax, and the Port has increased their level steadily over the years, it is likely this finding by Peat Marwick holds true today. Another finding in that report pointed out the Port received a total of 70 million in net government support that year. The Port staff member quoted in the article was obviously agitated by that figure and claimed it must be overstated. My opinion is that 70 million was a little too close to reported profits for the year which would tend to negate some of their economic benefit boasting. It would be several years later I would read a European report that claimed there is little or no economic benefit once all subsidies, tax breaks and other government support are calculated against so called profits for the Netherland airport of study.[16]

It isn't enough that the Port can collect property tax above the normal limit, or forcibly take property and be exempted from paying property tax on that property, lend credit which is prohibited by the state constitution for every government agency except for Port Districts, they are also allowed to start new taxes for industrial development. People living near the buy-out areas to the north and south of the airport are afraid of the types of business the Port might be inclined to attract in these vacant areas. Even though the Port is able to redevelop the land into open space or parkland, they have left most of it desolate for nearly 20 years with no foreseeable plans for re-use. Industrial development in the middle of neighborhoods where schools and retirement homes are the next most common land use besides homes does not seem compatible. In fact, it should be readily apparent to anyone objectively looking at this situation for the first time that it is the airport that is not compatible with the nearby land uses not the other way around.

Getting the airport to develop parks is another problem. When neighborhoods were bought out for the second runway back in the late 1960's, Evergreen Lake north of the airport was filled and the community surrounding the lake removed and cemented over. People on the west side lost their community center which included a pool and tennis court. The Port promised they would rebuild some of these facilities and parks. It took a huge effort on the part of many activists to get the park and community center started over 20 years later, and even then, it was mostly financed locally. At the last minute FAA withdrew the park funds they had contributed claiming they were not allowed (by their own rules apparently) to fund parks.

Sometime in the early 90's, 113 homeowners filed suit against the Port again claiming diminution. The judge made it clear that once a homeowner voluntarily entered into the noise program, they were no longer eligible for damages and he did not allow a class action. Individuals in the group who had never participated in the noise program settled with the Port after several years of negotiations. Others received damages accrued prior to entering the noise mitigation program. The firm retained by the homeowners had spent over a million dollars and they publicly announced they would never do it again.

Minnie also told me that the Port was granted governance over an area known as 6-6-1-1, six miles on either end of the runways and one mile on each side of the airport. When people living in this zone call their cities or county government for help, they are referred to the Port. They are their government.

With the virtual history tour Minnie had provided I was glad I had passed on the insulation program. She was happy to hear I had already got myself involved in a disagreement with the Port. Although reluctant to receive any new recruits because she had been let down by others in the past, she invited me to be a part of her group of three. Maybe I was naive or just plain stupid to think I could try to fight an agency with this much power, money and clout, and for thinking the fight would be fair, that they wouldn't lie cheat or manipulate information for their own benefit. But I wanted to be part of something so when Minnie invited me in, I was ready and willing to stick it out to the very end, whatever that might be.

I suppose my meeting with Minnie was a lot like airport 101 and the lessons would continue through the years. But although I had learned a lot about noise and the terrible way the Port was dealing with the problems their operations were creating for me and my family, Minnie was very interested in assigning me a project nobody else wanted but was sure would be an important issue. She had several reports on air pollution from jets she wanted me to look over I don't know why I said "sure" when she asked me if I wanted them. I took what she had, about a one foot tall pile of paper and left feeling like I had just had my first covert meeting with a spy in some kind of a secret war.

Chapter 4

JET AIR POLLUTION

Technical Report #58

I was anxious to get started on my assignment so first thing the next morning, I started to look through the reports Minnie had given me. The first was from 1970 by the Department of Commerce. This sounded very official to me. This report, I believe, was one of the first of its kind to look at airport emissions since the introduction of jets to commercial service, and was apparently prompted by community concern over the visible black smoke plume residents could see as planes approached and departed the airport. The study illustrated a fan shaped area of ground level affected by the jet emission plume which covered a 6 mile area for takeoffs and 12 miles from each runway end for landings and said:

> "On approach to thouchdown from the south, limits of pollution will extend from Auburn to Lake Killarney to Dash Point…Approaches from the north will disperse pollution over an area bounded by Eastgate, the original Lake Washington floating bridge, and northwestward to Alki Point lighthouse."[17]

The idea behind this schematic is that jet emissions have a ground level effect up to a certain height discussed by the industry as 2500 feet for takeoffs, twice this for landings. Above this, what is termed, "ceiling height", it is assumed that emissions mix with the atmosphere and disperse, generally not creating a ground level effect (the discussion never centers around the disposition of the soot, the heavier carbonaceous particulates that may have a ground level effect further than the ceiling). There is also debate about the ceiling height which varies from 2500 to 7500 feet.

This study discussed the use of "smokeless burner cans" which were supposed to dramatically reduce the visible black smoke. The dark cloud of soot is no longer as visible but as to whether it has actually been reduced has been a topic of discussion by at least two groups in this country who believe the smoke has been colored cloud white (metallic silver additive) rather than reduced. One New York based physician wrote:

> "6. The dense black smoke emissions that has discharged from jet aircraft have been disguised by an additive that lightens the color of the smoke to blend with the color of the sky."[18]

People living in the flight path still complain about residues coating their patio furniture and homes. Included amidst these reports was an article about a homeowner who lived about 1 mile from the runway end who was complaining of slimy deposits on his home. His street lines up with the end of the east runway, the longest of the two at Sea-Tac and taking most of the heavy jets departures:

> "If he had known about the heavy blanket of pollution falling daily from the sky, he said he would have chosen a different color for his house – a dark gray perhaps. 'I don't know what it is, but it's on everything I've got. The skylights in my house are just black'; he said. It takes the paint off cars and runs like oily slime down the side of his house when it

rains. 'This cherry tree', Mason said waving his arm, 'used to produce about three gallons. Last year I didn't even get enough to make a cherry pie. They're just all shriveled up.'

An inspector, Larry Vaughn from Puget Sound Clean Air Agency (formerly Puget Sound Air Pollution Control Agency) came to inspect the debirs and remarked:

"'I've seen similar situations in heavily industrialized areas'. But whether it's related to the airplanes or the traffic, or something being pulled in from the industrial areas – we'll just have to see.'"[19]

The Puget Sound Clean Air Agency, (PSCAA) operate regional particulate monitors, compile yearly air pollution data and issue permits for point sources. They took samples of this man's residues and found it to be fungal, organic material. Analysis of this soot has always been a political hot potato that in my opinion has not been properly addressed. Many jurisdictions around airports within the US have written resolutions concerned with the sooty deposits but since analysis seems to be contradictory, concern is never validated and the subject fades in and out of importance.

Every time I see an independent report on the soot, it is considered a very serious potential health threat. Reports produced by airports usually conclude there is either no soot or that it is something attributable to 'other' sources besides jets. I doubt the validity of these industry produced analyses due to the credible, although scant, contradictory reports that are available. There are far too many complaints about soot from residents in the jet flight paths and it is so unusual in the way it coats outdoor fixtures and runs off as black slime when washed for me to believe it is common or typical fungus. I have never trusted PSCAA since this time due to their, what I consider, dubious findings. I am also very concerned about the presence of polycyclic aromatic hydrocarbons (PAH), a by-product of jet fuel combustion, which can attach to the soot. I will talk about this more later on.

While living in the flight path, I had not noticed soot on my property before, but was living in the zone expected to be affected so I was now curious as to what was in the soot and whether it would cause health problems for people who might be exposed to breathing it.

Ecology

The second report from the State of Washington Department of Ecology (Ecology), the agency which oversees PSCAA, and who operates the Beacon Hill monitoring station, was dated 1991. I quickly read through this report and to my surprise, found out that jet emissions are not regulated, controlled or reported and they are HUGE! Criteria pollutants are controlled by standards called National Ambient Air Quality Standards (NAAQS) set by the US EPA. The inventories for criteria emissions totaled thousands of tons per year just for the jets. Criteria pollutants measured in this report included nitrogen dioxide (NO2) which is the brownish, poisonous gas most commonly associated with smog, expressed by the airport model used by Ecology in this report as nitrogen oxides (NOx) for which nitrogen dioxide is a part, sulfur dioxide (SO2), expressed in the report as sulfur oxides (SOx), carbon monoxide (CO), and particulates. Hydrocarbons which are not included in the NAAQS, include benzene, as well as a number of other compounds produced by jet combustion. Ozone is also covered by the NAAQS but not measured by the airport model. Ozone is produced when nitrogen oxides and hydrocarbons combine along with heat and time, although one obscure scientific analysis I no longer have discussed the possibility that ozone could be forming near the tarmac due to the heat of combustion and the high rate of the chemicals needed for formation. I have never made any headway arguing with the local air quality control agencies about this theory and to my knowledge no testing has ever been done around the airport for ozone.

Ecology's report predicted both nitrogen oxides in the form of nitrogen dioxide and particulates to be violating the federal standards.

Federal standards are set primarily to protect public health. Secondary standards, less strict than primary standards, are meant to protect the built and natural environment, trees, forests, etc. A predicted violation of a federal standard is serious business, especially since the region was out of compliance (non-attainment) from past violations of the ozone and carbon monoxide standards. These violations are considered a regional problem because monitoring for compliance is conducted on a regional level and federal money for any projects which might worsen non-attainment status or delay attainment is denied for the entire region when areas are in non-attainment, unless your plan includes extra bus lanes, bike paths or light rail. This is a real problem for the constrained Puget Sound region whose limited mobility corridors constantly need more lanes added to every highway and interstate.

According to Ecology, the high flame temperature of the newer jet engines, developed to reduce carbon monoxide and hydrocarbons is responsible for producing the extremely high rates of nitrogen oxides. Nitrogen oxides contribute to ozone. Ozone is regulated by the EPA because it is thought to cause serious health effects such as lung structure damage in young children, respiratory distress and is responsible for acidic rain, plant damage and a host of other environmental problems.

Tables of emission estimates in the appendix were taken directly from FAA's own data files used in the standard airport model, Emissions and Dispersion Modeling System (EDMS). From these tables I calculated that the two-minute takeoff of a DC-10 was equal to the emissions of nitrogen oxides of 21,530 cars in the same time period. Carbon monoxide from an idling 747 waiting for takeoff equals 8,000 cars pollution levels. I also noticed that there was a huge difference in the NOx inventory of all the cars coming to the airport at approximately 25.35 tons compared to jets at 2,066 tons and carbon monoxide, (CO) at 553 tons per year for cars and 3,440 for jets. We always hear that cars are the big pollution problem in the area, why haven't we ever heard anything about this jet emission problem before? If the cars are so bad, how is it that the planes that are thousands of times worse are ignored in the folklore? While cars are spread out all over the region, all these jets are operating right next to our neighborhoods and schools! Shouldn't someone be worried about this?

Apparently people began to talk about Ecology's report and get a little upset. The Ecology file Minnie had given me contained articles in the local paper quoting concerned citizens which also included a letter to the editor from Ecology. Responding to the citizen outrage, Ecology wanted to downplay the results saying it was only preliminary, don't worry, it's just a screening, merely an estimate of what might be out there, a more refined analysis would be needed that could use monitoring and modeling together to better determine what is really going on. I suppose if someone had questioned the reports credibility, Ecology would have gone out of their way to make it clear they used the airport's own facts, the FAA's model, accurate assumptions, their own technical experts and the best practices available, which was true. But because people were ready to panic when they read the report's conclusion about benzene, Ecology was on the hot seat to respond somehow. The report said:

> "Utilize the mobile monitor van to do some sampling in the areas around Sea-Tac Airport expected to have the highest impacts especially for benzene which, as discussed earlier, may pose a ***large risk*** to the nearby communities"[20] (emphasis added)

"...however, this screening study of Sea-Tac's emissions showed that the airport's contribution to ground-level pollutant concentrations is higher than expected."[21]
"The possibility of ambient air quality violations for nitrogen dioxide and particulates solely from Sea-Tac Airport contributions has been identified. It also appears that Sea-Tac is a significant contributor of hydrocarbons and carbon monoxide, and, to a lesser degree, of sulfur oxides."[22]

They noted Seattle Christian School might be experiencing some of the highest peaks of airborne benzene emissions. This school was subsequently bought by the Port for an airline office building and a new school was built a mile to the northeast of the airport. Benzene is suspected to cause myeloid leukemia, Hodgkins, disease and lymphoma.[23]

Included in with the papers Minnie had given me was a newspaper clipping about emission estimates from Frankfurt which generally agreed with the total emission inventories from Ecology which said:

"During take-off and acceleration, there is an emission of mostly nitrogen oxides. During landing, CO is emitted in addition to nitrogen oxides. For the year 1984, for example, it is estimated that 84% of the CO 90% of the hydrocarbons, and 70% of the nitrogen oxides emitted by air traffic are produced below the altitude of 10 kilometers. Given these factors, air traffic pollutes mainly in the areas surrounding the airport. For the densely populated area surrounding Frankfurt, the yearly emissions of CO was 3,528 tons. This corresponds to the CO emissions of all motor vehicles which, in the same year, were on the road in the Frankfurt area. Especially in these densely populated areas, air traffic contributes heavily to the increases in the previously mentioned pollutants, as well as increasing the level of smog. CO and nitrogen oxides are responsible for the formation of peroxyacetylnitrates, the so-called PAN-combinations, and catalyze the formation of ozone in the lower layers of the atmosphere – the troposphere. Ozone, as well as the PAN-combinations, irritate mucous membranes and damage plants."[24]

MIDWAY

The third report Minnie gave me was a 1993 EPA report of Midway Airport hydrocarbon and particulate emissions in a format to discover cancer risk for nearby residents. This report, like the Ecology report I had looked through, concluded there is risk. The main culprit from this report though was 1,3-butadiene from jet emissions which hadn't even been discussed for Sea-Tac in Ecology's report. In direct contradiction to nearly every industry produced document for Sea-Tac claiming cars are the primary culprit of concern, Midway's study concluded;

> "Overall, emissions from aircraft operated at Midway in 1990 contribute up to 99% of the total cancer cases. This was expected since the vehicular emissions estimated at Midway are insignificant compared to the aircraft emissions at Midway."[25]

The estimates for local industrial facilities (which, by the way, was the primary target of concern with constituency pressure put onto local elected officials initiating the look into risk at Midway in the first place), were reported in the pounds per year while the airport's jet inventory was reported in tons per year. Particulates from just the jets at Midway were 48.87 tons per year, with all cars at 0.068. Ecology's report had jet particulate at 67 tons per year and cars at .13. By the time Sea-Tac issued their draft Environmental Impact Statement (EIS) for the third runway project in 1996, all particulate for jets would mysteriously have disappeared from the model.

Nobody would dare call this EPA study which used the same model as Ecology's screening analysis, preliminary or shoddy, needing more validation. This was a very thorough, technically sound, sophisticated and complex study. Grid points were on a two dimensional box graph charting risk factors. I am fairly certain that this was the most accurate computer modeling of an airport's emission risks to date which not only used modeling but also monitoring for validation, and then attached risk estimates to each compound using EPA data. This report agreed with the basic conclusions of Ecology's report, the emissions are huge and expected to cause what one analyst found to be at least a 10% higher cancer risk in nearby and downwind communities.

I realized now that I was probably living near one of the most dangerous polluters in the state. Particulates violating the standard, possibly giving us heart and lung disease, maybe carrying toxic particles that could cause cancer, benzene, 1,3 butadiene, formaldehyde, ozone, the brown cloud of nitrogen dioxide that you could even see from a distance hanging over our communities, who knows what kind of toxic chemical zoo was here, nobody was checking! This combined with noise violating EPA standards, probably weakening us, maybe the combination of noise and air pollution destroying our ability to fight disease...who knows?

Minnie told me that the Port was working on a sampling study soon to be released which would include benzene and provided me with a copy after months of trying to obtain it from the Port of Seattle.

MFG

Since Ecology had nearly bent over backwards to downplay community concern by almost debunking their own study in 1991, claiming more analysis was needed, the Port was under some pressure to do more to either dispel or validate community concern.

McCulley, Frick & Gilman (MFG) was hired by the Port and gathered hydrocarbon samples on four days on and off airport property for 8 hours each day in October through December 1993. They used credible EPA approved methods and samplers, quality control, included wind, temperature and overall weather conditions. Rates of certain chemicals, formaldehyde, acetaldehyde, acrolein, dichloromethane, carbon tetrachloride and trichloroethylene were found to be above the Acceptable Source Impact Level (ASIL). The ASIL is used by PSCAA when they issue permits for smoke stacks. If a facility is predicted or monitored above the ASIL, a permit will not be issued or withdrawn until scrubbers or other 'best management practice' (BMP) devices can be affixed to reduce emissions to allowable levels. As Ecology had predicted, benzene was also monitored above the ASIL. Both benzene and formaldehyde were 50 times higher. If Sea-Tac were a smokestack, it could not be permitted to operate. The ASIL, however, doesn't apply to Sea-Tac simply because it is not a smokestack and there are presently no source regulations for an airport.

I began to gather information on the effects of some of these chemicals and found that they cause skin and eye irritation, dizziness, liver effects, mutations, tumors, lymphoma, lung, throat and nasal irritation, cancer and suspected to cause brain tumors among other things.

Many legislative attempts by airport groups around the country have been made over the past two decades to enact or pass a bubble bill which would require states and/or local air pollution agencies to regulate all emissions inside airport property as though they were a smokestack. These attempts so far have been vehemently opposed probably because disclosure of emissions, heretofore kept well hidden, could cause the industry to make changes they are not ready or willing to make.

When I spoke with PSCAA about the MFG results, they assured me the state source limits (ASIL) are set at levels meant to be overprotective so they were not too concerned. They pointed out that the MFG survey, which some people affectionately began to call the "frick-n gilman," was for only 8 hours each day and a yearly figure from an 8 hour sample was not regularly used to compare to an annual ASIL. Sampling would have to be done for an entire year before anyone could make a proper comparison, but even then, PSCAA couldn't do anything because the airport is not a smokestack. A study this long would cost over a million dollars, which was still a lot of money in 1993. I pointed out that the 8 hour sample of acrolein was **334** times higher than the **24-hour ASIL,** and they were sure I was wrong and would have to see the report. Formaldehyde was 47 times higher, benzene 53 times higher, but still, they couldn't do anything because they didn't regulate the airport.

Annual inventory rates of three cancer causing chemicals at Midway Airport totaled 9 tons for benzene, 7.6 tons of 1,3 butadiene (not measured at Sea-Tac, but causing the most cancer risk increase at Midway) and a whopping 63 tons of formaldehyde. A senior scientist at US EPA said of levels detected at Midway Airport:

> "The formaldehyde is a mind blower compared to the other industries on a local basis. It's the kind of thing that should have been flagged,"[26]

Since the days were typical and weather indicated no inversion or circumstances for unusually high pollution levels, averaging the 8 hour samples to equal a yearly average didn't seem like a leap of stupidity to me. The airport, unlike typical smokestacks, operates 24 hours a day. There is no reason to believe these averages wouldn't be present all year long. But the regulators disagreed and scolded me for inappropriately trying to convert averages. Funny how Ecology concluded more should be done because their study was only a screening and when that happened, MFG concluded everything was fine until I pointed out that was an incorrect conclusion, and then it was called too short term. Make up your minds.

I decided to call the King County Department of Public Health (KCDPH) and inform them of the dangers we were living with. They seemed interested in the results and so I spent quite a bit of time typing a summary of my concerns about the report and mailed them a copy of the survey along with my summary. I pointed out that our area of residences, schools, retirement facilities, churches and nursing homes had been compared by MFG to the most polluted industrial areas of the country during the highest pollution episodes concluding we are; "within the range observed in other urban areas."[27] I had a concern the studies used for comparison from Houston, Atlanta and Dallas could have been heavily influenced by nearby airport pollution problems, with Atlanta and Dallas having two of the busiest airports in the country. In essence, our oversaturated area heavily influenced by jet emissions may have been being compared to the same problem. About a month later I got a letter from the Chief saying he had sent my summary to the Port of Seattle to consider during their third runway proposal. I was completely shocked when I read this, especially since I had nothing nice to say about the consultants' conclusions. Health of the people exposed to this pollution load, I thought, should be a concern for the department. Instead, they thought they should tell the polluter they are polluting as if they didn't know already. I was embarrassed that my scathing summary was handed to the Port like classmates notes being handed to the teacher. I never trusted KCDPH after this and they would be of no further assistance to me in the future.

So now, with three reports on Sea-Tac that I was aware of, one was too old to be of any value, one was only a screening and the latest, too short term to be considered useful. Nobody wanted to talk about the Midway report. Each in the succession stressed the need for more analysis. What is enough? This one says it is bad, but we need to know how bad or how, how bad or what? If someone says you should do a better study, why spend the money on another study that also demands more studies? But while I was ranting to people about the high rates of cancer causing emissions and illness causing criteria pollutants, the Port was busy telling people that everything was good. Who are you going to believe, a homemaker from Des Moines with relatively no emission background or credentials or 10 degreed businessmen in suits at the next meeting in DC? I supposed I needed credibility and, apparently, a butt load of more studies.

My kitchen table was starting to look a lot like Minnie's. I had a stack of papers about one foot high at all times. For credibility, I wasn't sure if I needed to be an air pollution engineer, or some kind of a medical detective but I continued my course in digesting information, finding it enjoyable but absolutely not a simple, shoot the breeze topic for discussion with my friends, family or neighbors.

Meanwhile, the airport was getting ready to launch its environmental impact statement for the third runway. Minnie's group was busy gathering as much information as they could on things that could put the whammy on the Port's plans. I was getting up at 6 a.m. and began my program of reading any air pollution information I could find. I was somewhat surprised that I was able to understand a lot of it too. I didn't know why I was doing this either. Maybe I would use it for something someday, but I didn't know what or when that would be.

Since I believed I should begin to share this information with the community, I started attending the CASE meetings regularly and ran into someone who became very influential over my life, a nice lady named Pat.

Chapter 5

CASE

Citizens Against Sea-Tac Expansion, (CASE) had been growing and in 1995, held monthly meetings at the local school district headquarters which had a large meeting room that could seat 100 people. Helen and Pat were in charge of cookies, coffee and setting out flyers, copies of news articles and information on the big table at the back of the room. Helen's husband had been a pilot but was now passed away. Helen would often talk about the days when flying was a luxury not many people could afford and how it had turned into a regular transportation mode that nearly anyone could use. I suppose if you have an airport in the middle of a lower income area and only the rich can afford to fly, it probably seems unfair to burden the less privileged with the noise and pollution from the uses of the privileged. But it only makes all the problems worse if it accommodates everybody because the busier the airport, the more the impact on those communities.

Pat is a good cook and a real nice person who had an obvious desire to accomplish something good out of all this. I liked her instantly. At one of the summer meetings at a fire station when the school district was closed, she came up to me while I was sitting in the audience and grabbed my arm and said; "get up there and talk." I said; "What are you talking about?" She said;

36

"he (the speaker) is boring them to death, look, they're all falling asleep." Since most of the crowd was elderly, this probably wasn't that unusual, but I didn't really know what to do so I continued to sit there and shake my head. At the end of the meeting, Pat asked me to run for CASE president at the next election in January. With complete false confidence I said sure, once again obligating myself to something I knew nothing about. This group actually had about 3,000 members on their books, although it was only a handful of people who were very active and maybe 100 would regularly attend the monthly meetings. The battle against another runway was heating up and residents were increasingly frustrated and angry, the leader of this group at this time in history would take the heat for losing or be congratulated for winning. I really didn't want to be responsible for either. But I was ready and willing to fight like mad and it seemed like a good idea to trust Pat's judgment since she had been in the group for many years.

Many of the people attending these monthly meetings were residents of Normandy Park, one of the four little cities which encompass the airport. Normandy Park is a community located near the Puget Sound and the hills slope gradually toward the water which creates a lot of view properties. The homes are beautiful and the lots are large by ordinance. Average home price in 2004 was 300,000, compared to Burien, just to the north at 174,000. Many residents of Normandy Park work for Boeing and many also regularly attended the CASE meetings, although many of the attendees were retired. I thought the CASE group would have a lot of clout with so many professionals in their membership. Many politicians have at some time in their careers attended our meetings, looking for support and making promises. Unlike Normandy Park residents who would be newly affected and some more affected by a third runway, my situation was a little different. I would not be newly affected by a third runway, I was already being affected by the first and second runway. I wasn't fighting against what was coming, I was angry about what was already there. Maybe that anger gave me more tenacity and that is what Pat liked.

As January approached, Pat once again asked me to run for CASE president. I am not sure what she saw in me that made her think I was the right person for the job. I would be replacing an acting councilmember and hardly seemed qualified, but if I could get enough of the right people to work with me, maybe I could pull it off by hiding behind their work. Pat assured me she would do everything she could to make this successful. She pointed out how important it would be to have young people involved who could bring energy to the group.

At the beginning of December 1995, I was elected CASE president to begin serving a one year term starting in January 1996. I was very excited about the unanimous vote, but in retrospect I really don't think anyone else was running. In fact, probably nobody else wanted to, but I didn't know that. I was just happy to know someone thought I could do something.

Three of the four board members would continue, but the secretary, Tonya would be moving on to a new job. Pat told me I should ask another young person in the group, David, to be my secretary. I knew who he was from seeing him and his young son at meetings, but wondered whether he would want to make a commitment to write minutes, agendas and make arrangements for the group. I begged Pat to ask him for me but she insisted I do it so I called David and asked him. He said he would have to think about it. I told him the group wanted young people. He then instantly agreed. Jim who had retired from the FAA agreed to continue as the vice-president and Wally would be treasurer.

I suppose my functions as president of this activist group could be summarized with the following; "God help us all! Although it seemed like our primary purpose as a group was to fight the upcoming expansion of the airport from two to three runways, surely there were very few people who believed we had a chance. Most people probably came to meetings for Pat's delicious cookies, and something to do on a Wednesday night.

One of my first projects as President was to attempt to educate the members on the dangers of the jet air pollution. Most of my presentations were met with deer in the headlights blank stares. Nobody asked any questions. I told them nobody was in charge. Nobody is protecting you. We need to call them. People asked who to call and what to say. But people were afraid. They hadn't sat at their kitchen table and in the library or with doctors and engineers for the past year or so like I had and what was simple now for me was a complete foreign language to my group. I did manage to get them involved in a protest at the airport where about 20 people showed up. We put on gas masks, held signs and marched up and down the sidewalk for about two hours. The media came and reluctantly printed a few sentences about the protest they surmised must be nothing more than an awareness building event. Nobody printed anything about the signs which said things like; "Jet pollution kills" and "One jet takeoff = the pollution level of 21,530 cars."

One of the hotel staff offered us a complimentary snack at their restaurant if we purchased a meal. A few cars honked their horns at us. Some of the group complained about the hot breath steam inside their gas masks and then we got done and went home. It was just another typical day in the lives of some crazy senior citizens.

At our regular CASE meetings, I invited guests to talk about the upcoming process for the third runway. We had local and federal representatives update us on what was happening on a local and national level. Many times during my first year as president, people running for office would ask for our endorsement. I directed our board to accept everyone in who wanted to come and talk, but cautioned them to never endorse a particular candidate as a group. We had members from all walks of the political spectrum; our board was mostly conservative with many general members democrat. We always got along great though since we had the one issue in common but I believed endorsing someone could damage our unity.

Randy Tate as 9th District Congressman actually brought the Federal Aviation Subcommittee to Des Moines Field House for a hearing. When the meeting time approached, the airport suddenly switched to north flow, meaning the sub-committee wouldn't have the chance to be interrupted or shocked by the loud takeoff noise over this 1939 un-insulated historic landmark in the flight path above 65 DNL. Was the switch necessary or malicious? Port officials were present at this packed meeting and during the hearing, Congressman Tate held the Sea-Tac aviation director Gina Marie Lindsey's feet to the fire about whether the Port would raise taxes to fund construction of the third runway. He asked her several times. Each time she denied it. The last time he asked her she admitted they might have to. All along, the Port had always claimed none of their tax revenue is used to support the airport and in no way was it intended to be used to pay for the third runway. Construction would be funded by user fees, federal funds, bond issuance and other, as yet, unidentified, means.

According to the Port, nearly all 64 million of the Port's annual tax collection in 1995 went mainly to cover losses at the seaport. This cannot be verified because taxes go into a pot called 'non-operating revenue' which has no general accounting of expenses as is evident from the research council's analysis of Port expenses discussed earlier. But the expense of the runway was going to be huge and federal subsidy could run into the billions. Congressman Tate wanted the subcommittee to hear not only the high price tag but that the Port did not yet have a plan in place to pay for it.

Congressman Tate continued to visit our community group and appeared to work very hard for the 'cause'. As the next election drew near however, one of the more vocal activists in our CASE group insisted we endorse a different candidate, Adam Smith. I reminded her that our group philosophy was to support everyone who wanted to help us, but endorse no one. This caused a small rift in our otherwise happy little camp. Why endorse someone just because he's a democrat when he has no history of representing our interests, while a tried and true incumbent who happens to be in the 'other' party does? Nobody would really care what issue or what party stopped expansion. Whether environmental issues or financial boondoggle, who cares?

I think people assume that because you are a democrat that you must care for the environment. We had several members in our CASE group who were republicans who cared about the environment, and several democrats who cared about the ridiculous cost of the 8,500 foot pavement. We also appealed to elected environmental democrats who never helped us and fiscally conservative republicans who likewise dismissed our concerns. A balance between business profits and healthy consumers doesn't need party affiliation, it's just plain common sense. For thousands of years people have managed to spare the earth for us to use, yet in a mere half century we've raped, pillaged and plundered the planet like there's no tomorrow. I think that is irresponsible. Doesn't matter if you are a democrat or republican, environmentalist or gun-toting red neck, drinking poisoned water and breathing polluted air is bad no matter what your affiliation.

The vocal member publicly announced our group endorsement favoring Adam Smith despite my previous warnings. Temporarily, I had to do some damage control since none of this was done by direction of the board or membership. Randy Tate barely lost and the new congressman did not follow through on things Tate had started. This would not be the last time our group was used for individuals' own personal ideas rather than by member consensus.

Chapter 6

PSRC

The Puget Sound Regional Council, (PSRC) is a state appointed group of officials representing the region on transportation planning. They were in charge of deciding whether to approve a new third parallel runway at Sea-Tac or expand somewhere else.

The PSRC initially looked at a number of alternative airport and runway sites in the region including Paine Field in Snohomish County near Everett to the north and McChord Air Force Base in Pierce County to the south as well as expanding Sea-Tac in King County, in the middle of the region.

Paine Field was dropped from the list because, according to one report, there were far too many wetlands which would be affected at Paine and a terminal would need to be built or expanded. The same report said Sea-Tac would be the better option because there would be no wetland impacts and although this turned out to be wrong, nobody was on board to say Paine looks like a better option because the wetlands turned out to be equal and the cost at Paine would be about a billion dollars cheaper. Nope. McChord was dropped once it became apparent the military wasn't willing to give up their base yet. Well, duh. Who would have thought this was a good option in the beginning when an active military is still working there? So that left Sea-Tac, which was actually required to be used by the same legislation that created the PSRC in the first place mandating they stick to existing facilities rather than citing new ones.

The PSRC felt a little sorry for the folks living around Sea-Tac, since we squealed like pigs as loud as the rest of the communities near Paine and McChord. So when it became apparent they were going to shove it on us like they had planned all along, they passed a resolution. They would only approve a third runway at Sea-Tac if an expert noise panel, completely independent of airport interests and appointed by the State of Washington, would find that noise had been reduced by the Port's really expensive noise insulation programs.

A three member panel, including a noise expert and an attorney, were chosen and they took testimony from a packed auditorium of nearly 1,000 residents. They received vast amounts of data from the Port and deliberated for over a year. During this process they conducted a telephone survey of various residents asking if they were satisfied with the noise insulation and whether they felt they had experienced meaningful relief. Overwhelmingly, the residents were dissatisfied. Minnie supplied the panel with a picture of one of the Port's noise monitors that although had generated data, was not connected to anything. Bare wires were dangling from the equipment. Their final decision on noise issues was released in April 1996. The majority ruled noise had not been reduced.

I remember that when the headline hit the local newspaper, everyone in the communities surrounding the airport was jubilant. We were 100% confident that the runway was now dead. We could relax.

The majority of the panel, who found the Port had not succeeded in meaningful noise reduction, had recommended a number of things the Port could have done or could do to actually achieve this goal, however they were also sure that increased operations in the future would offset any gains. They recommended the Port more aggressively advertise their programs, especially transaction assistance, conduct further buy-out of properties and consider a greater level of insulation. The expert panel had also said the Port was not as cooperative as they could have been, sometimes supplying more data than necessary, the wrong data, or delaying their response to the Panel's requests for data.

So while the communities were busy celebrating, the PSRC was preparing their response to these findings. Their own resolution had tied their hands. They could not authorize a third runway and this approval was needed for the Port to proceed.

The PSRC is an odd group. They are all elected officials, representing everyone in the region, while representing nobody at all. They are county executives and council members and in their normal capacity representing their city or county, they make executive decisions to approve or not approve things, decisions which have consequences for the people of their district and usually should not affect people in another jurisdiction. As PSRC these individuals represent transportation planning for the four county region which can have an effect on people inside and outside their jurisdiction. So if they have 100 members, only 3 or 4 might be appointed or chosen who represent the people living near the airport. If the PSRC votes to put in another runway at Sea-Tac, the vote will be 97 in favor and 3 against. If they vote to expand Paine Field, the vote will be 97 in favor and 3 against. It is the same for prisons, sewage treatment plants and waste facilities. Nobody wants these "essential public facilities" built near their homes so they are cited by special purpose governance. This keeps the heat off the local official who votes no and spread out far enough through the majority that nobody is accountable.

PSRC at least had the decency to wait a week while we celebrated like fools before announcing they were rewriting their resolution. The new resolution said the Port could build a runway if they incorporated some of the recommendations from the expert panel into their upcoming planning processes without specifying which ones, when, how or who would pay for them. They also included wording that made it appear that the legislature should write some laws providing we, the dumb victims of their political wrangling, should be compensated. Some time later, they would drop this clause claiming they had no power to influence the state legislative process. Funny how all the representatives and county executives in the most populated counties in the state can get together and do just about anything they want, but when it comes to trying to lobby for legislation, they are helpless.

The expert panel had made it clear that nothing had worked well enough up until now. The Port had advertised their insulation program as the best in the country. How much more can you do besides blowing a thousand pounds of guck into the walls of homes and separating their window panes by four inches? Can you add more layers? Maybe you can put double triple pane windows onto a home. They cannot be opened, but maybe this is all the better? Maybe they could wrap the whole house in bubble wrap and make it a little quieter? Pretty soon, you get so sealed up in the house, maybe you can't get out. What kind of life is this? Once you cut your way out into your yard, you still can't talk to anyone without being interrupted every 20 seconds by the drone of jet engines as plane after plane goes overhead. Since the noise doesn't completely die down between jets, as the airport gets busier, you might eventually have to wait an hour between sentences until peak departure is over.

The PSRC held a public meeting to spring the good news of how much more we could expect from the Port in the way of insulation. I had arranged for some of the CASE members to hold signs outside and some of us planned to disrupt the meeting inside. We sent out press releases. But who could stop them? Certainly, the constituency in Kitsap County 50 miles away from Sea-Tac isn't going to come after their representative for changing the resolution. Do you think the single councilmember from Des Moines is going to muscle his way through to convince the rest to stick to their word? Is the media going to report that a bunch of representatives acted inappropriately? They might if it didn't happen so often. I had included in the press release that we might disrupt and apparently although no media showed up, the assembly was ready for this with extra police on hand.

During the meeting I shouted out that they were liars for going back on their word. Our future state Governor, Gary Locke, who now works for President Obama, who CASE had endorsed for King County Executive years earlier because he promised if elected, would vote against the runway, was in the group that I called murderers. He voted against us at every opportunity. I said people would get sick and maybe even die from airport operations and that the PSRC would be responsible for every death from here on. A representative from another county came over to me and warned me that my group had better behave ourselves or we would be thrown out by the police. I yelled even more and several police crouded around me all at once telling me to leave but were ready to carry me out if I didn't cooperate. The rest of the group, who had also agreed to be disruptive, sat politely and quietly while PSRC proceeded to read our sentence. Nobody in my group noticed I was physically escorted outside. They asked me later why I had left. I reminded them that we were going to get a little crazy. Apparently they had forgotten.

No reporters had showed up to report that this nicest group of mostly elderly people who were so ready to apologize to everyone for disrupting the meeting were lied to. At the end of the meeting, everyone got up shuffled out, got onto the bus we had rented and went home to our own personal kerosene chambers. Granted, it might have looked like only the weak, the frail and elderly were upset but what else could we do. The younger people living in the area are at work at 3:00 in the afternoon when they hold these meetings. It's the retirees and homemakers fighting for everyone in the afternoon. Since there aren't many homemakers left and the retirees aren't going to throw themselves into the path of the speeding bureaucracy we might appear weak, especially when the process goes on for years. People get tired.

The PSRC process looking for other airport sites was met with large crowds of people who probably took the day off work. Angry residents came out in droves to oppose Paine Field expansion. Essentially Paine Field at any moment could be receiving more commercial service since it has received FAA funding in the past, but Sea-Tac has a lock on service and therefore, revenue that they are not willing to share.

Alternative airport citing is merely a diversion tactic that is played out all over. It is a prerequisite for regional transportation planning to receive federal funds, but still a useless and meaningless endeavor after all. I don't believe there was ever any plan to open Paine Field to commercial service or transform McChord from Military use. In my opinion, this is just one more way to sidetrack the public pressure from the real plan while gaining more pressure from outside areas to push for Sea-Tac expansion. My group was so angry that Paine Field was dropped and Paine Field residents, I am sure, were as happy as clams that Sea-Tac was being expanded instead. I believe airports and the FAA laugh at the way they get communities to fight each other rather than them, the real enemy.

Every time the Sydney residents would get riled up over a third runway at KSA, officials would pull out their trump card of a reliever airport at Badgery's Creek. This would distract everyone for awhile, just long enough to secretly push the knife a little deeper into the chest of the communities suffering from KSA. They would then drop the issue. According to Paul Fitzgerald, in 10 years of talking about a new airport at Badgery's, their only progress was to turn one shovel. City of Chicago, who owns and operates O'Hare, has been talking about a new airport at Peotone for at least 10 years now. As far as I know, no shovels at all have been turned there. Here, they are still discussing Paine Field and a new airport from time to time but shovels haven't even been bought. These airports are not a reliever for what is already there either. I believe they are in addition to what is already there. If anything, they will take the light aircraft from Sea-Tac and O'Hare and put more heavy jets over our homes. The light aircraft at Sea-Tac is the only thing keeping the community half sane. But there is probably no real plan for these other airports to open or expand their service in the first place. The hubs have a lock and key on the monopoly and are not about to give up one bit of service transferring cargo and passenger dollars to any other municipality.

One of the airlines using Sea-Tac recently wanted to move to Boeing field because it was financially more appealing. The county voted not to allow it even though Boeing Field is more than adequate to accommodate commercial service. It isn't about convenience or crowding. It's about money and power and control.

Even though we had lost with the PSRC decision, we still had the ongoing EIS process and I believed I had a chance with the numbers of people in CASE, to make a dent in the process and get officials and regulators to pay attention to what I believed to be the worst threat to our communities, jet produced emissions.

Chapter 7

GOT ANY GUM?

The bible on the left is dwarfed by the three volume Sea-Tac Airport Master Plan Update Environmental Impact Statement.

The Port released their Draft Environmental Impact Statement (EIS) which was also a Master Plan Update April 1995. I was shocked at its size. We had 30 days to comment on this massive document. How could someone read, research, understand and comment on this in just 30 days? Even if you didn't have a job, reading just one of the three volumes could take several weeks. There are footnotes everywhere that need research, references to check, prior data and models to look through.

For every 100 pages of meaningless meanderings of how the beautiful airport is so special, there were about 10 paragraphs of important information tucked away. You had to be a genius to find it. For instance, one seemingly misplaced paragraph in the draft said the Port and FAA were waiting to hear from residents in the new flight path to know whether they wanted to be bought out. In the final EIS another obscure paragraph said they didn't hear from anyone so assumed they wanted to stay.

Most people were not equipped to notice a problem in the readout graphs from the air pollution modeling or see a discrepancy with the noise monitor #2 readout data from January 12. Others wouldn't notice fudged numbers from outfall number #4 in relationship to the water discharge permit. But there were people in our group who did know these things and they did comment and their comments were good. But they were no more successful than John Q. Public who said the noise is bothering me and I cannot sleep well at night. No meaningful changes were made to the manuscript as a result of comments.

One of the big problems with the whole set up is that the Port creates the data, and uses their own standards for scrutiny. There is no independent third party to say if the assumptions, methods or conclusions are right or wrong. EPA, Ecology and PSCAA were all involved with scoping before the EIS was written and they each asked for certain things to be included. When they weren't, the process still moved forward as though the agencies either forgot what they asked for or no longer cared. When they asked a second and third time and it still wasn't included, the text would state it had been done earlier.

At some point, when the EIS is final, there are no more chances for a reiteration that certain things were never done. Detangling the web of information through thousands of pages of dubious meanderings, vague references and tricky distortions by the consultant, Landrum & Brown is nearly impossible. In my opinion, the consultant, who is hired and paid by the Port to write the EIS, should be considered in collusion and disqualified. Instead they are congratulated for coming up with such a comprehensive document.

Not knowing how complicated this was going to become and being the new baby expert in a field that nobody else wanted, I was excited to get started pulling apart the air quality. Minnie bought a copy of the EIS and arranged a meeting for her group, myself, Pat, Helen, Rose and Audrey to take parts home to work on. I took air quality and Rose and Audrey took the section on human health because they had been working on a cancer map.

The EIS began by stating its purpose and need to "Alleviate bad weather delay by building a dependent all purpose runway." Gulp, what?

This was the first time any of us had heard that bad weather delay was a problem at Sea-Tac. The EIS boasted a 44% bad weather delay problem. Why didn't they just say they wanted to increase capacity? All documents leading up to this event had said the region needed to increase capacity as aviation demand was on the rise. But now, we were all seeing for the first time that Sea-Tac was somehow socked in with a horrible fog problem none of us had known, heard or seen before. None of us believed it either. We had pilots and many frequent travelers in our CASE group who claimed Sea-Tac, in their experience, was one of the least delayed airports in the country.

The third runway would be spaced 2500 feet from the first, which we had known beforehand, but we didn't know it would be dependent, in other words, there would still need to be separation between landing aircraft in poor weather. Simultaneous landings in poor weather would not be safe. So why build it? If separation was the purpose, and not capacity increase, we asked why not move the second runway over.

A copy of one of FAA's advisory documents said runway separation for completely independent landings in poor weather needed to be 4300 feet, but dual simultaneous departures 2500 feet, the exact separation planned for the third runway. I thought this was suspicious. I asked several times through the process whether simultaneous departure was the real reason behind the runway and the Port denied it. Any moron would guess they wanted this separation for dual simultaneous departures, maybe during peak hour in the morning because that is the exact distance required by FAA. They wouldn't admit it though and maybe they had a reason. Fog is a safety issue. Delays are a costs issue. Peak hour is only for spoiled airlines who want it all.

The full build out which included a terminal, drives, gates, parking expansion, roadway access improvements, home purchase, demolition and mitigation was estimated to cost around 3 billion dollars. This was before the cost of the runway doubled to one billion by itself over the next several years. Denver had been building an entire new airport with 6 runways on 64,000 acres for a total cost of 4 billion. Why would we add just one runway for almost the same cost as an entire new airport? And have that runway be dependent, too short for most takeoffs, with a short term benefit for foggy delays that didn't even occur here?

The preposterous expensive runway was only part of the overall lunacy. A huge valley would need to be filled with dirt making it the second largest dirt hauling project in state history, just behind Grand Coulee dam. At one peak on the runway plateau, a material stabilized engineered wall would rise over 200 feet. According to an engineer in the CASE group, it would then be one of the highest in the country. The runway itself was already being discussed as the most expensive single runway in US history. One hundred businesses and 350 single family homes and apartments would have to be mowed down to make way for the dirt. Miller Creek, an endangered salmon bearing stream would have to be relocated. At the time the EIS was written they estimated less than 10 acres of wetlands would be destroyed with the dirt, this figure would double once all the properties had been purchased. Another 18 acres of wetlands to the north of the airport was slated for a new parking lot. EPA put the kibosh on that once the wetland acreage destruction for the runway rose up to 13. A roadway expansion by the State would affect another 10 acres of wetlands and along the way, one acre would be filled, here, another there, piecemeal to keep agencies from noticing a huge total. Paine Fields' exaggerated losses of wetlands compared to Sea-Tac's vastly understated estimates certainly played a deceptive role in the planning process. But who is there to correct these?

Other chapters of the EIS document covered effects to human health, but only a cursory overview…far more information would be needed. They intended to mine the buy-out area to the south of the airport, as though it wasn't a desolate enough wasteland already. The appearance of this area is so unusual. You can see remnants of streets and elaborate plants which used to be part of landscaped yards. Grasses had grown up in every cement crack and the absence of the homes amidst the un-kept yards behind the barbed wire fence makes it look like a ghost town without the town.

The construction plan included a separate proposal to barge fill in from Maury Island to Des Moines. This would require building a barge dock at the Des Moines Beach Park. Part of the proposal plan to build a conveyor belt to carry dirt more than a mile from the beach to the runway area was met with huge opposition by residents. Years later, a scandal erupted over the conveyor. The Mayor of Des Moines and a councilmember resigned because it became known that a large, partially undisclosed, contribution to their campaigns came from the company who had proposed the conveyor system.

Endangered species habitat would be removed. Falcon, frog and fox were to lose their foraging area and they would have to find a new one on their own or die. An endangered species impact zone was drawn on a map in the EIS shaped like a rectangle everywhere around the airport except for a notched corner leaving out a known bald eagles nest where no impact was expected to the nesting endangered bird and its family.

There would be water, ground, surface runoff, floodplain impacts. The top layer of the aquifer under the airport was already admittedly contaminated with several feet of jet fuel. The underground jet fuel lines were corroded and leaking according to Ecology. Hydrant lines needed to be replaced. Fuel tanks buried under hangars were suspected to be leaking. All this sits atop a large aquifer on a plateau with several creeks draining the waste into the Puget Sound. At the time, two water districts drew from the middle part of this Highline Aquifer for drinking water for residential use. In summer months, city of Seattle supplemented with Highline aquifer water although they said it was poor quality and needed to be blended. Experts testified that there are holes between the first and second aquifer while others who derive or expect to receive income from the Port claimed it was separated by an impermeable layer. I think the fact that you have to bore through the top to get to the lower levels would indicate there might be a hole.

Although many of these issues were included in scoping comments from Ecology before the official comment period, (scoping is where the agencies give input to the consultants for methodology and items to include in the Environmental Impact Statement) Ecology would not formally submit comments on the project making them ineligible to approve or disapprove of the final document. This meant there would be no regulatory input on the projects compliance with state environmental law which mirrors the federal requirements.

There would be attempts to fill the plateau area with contaminated dirt. About the time our CASE group learned the

Port planned to use contaminated dirt, we also learned the Port was engaged in trying to change the state law to allow it. This attempt ultimately failed after citizens worked very hard and spent countless hours fighting the change. If we hadn't learned by coincidence of the attempt when we did, it would have passed. Citizens would have to watchdog the Port's use of water as they had suggested using Highline Water District resources on site which the district considered theft. Several hundred thousand gallons had recently disappeared from this currently unused capped well. The district blamed the Port but the Port denied it. Even though access was limited to the district and the Port, there was no way to pin down exactly who had used the water or for what reason so the matter was dropped. Mining would need a permit from the state which was at one time unwilling to issue this without serious restrictions on cuts, depths and duration of open pits. The Army Corps would have to permit a less than normal replacement ratio for a higher than normal number of wetland acres and allow out of basin mitigation, another unusual practice not normally allowed. The Port wanted to create new wetlands in the city of Auburn, fifteen miles to the south of the airport. The EPA would have to approve the project for Air and Water Quality under the Clean Air and Water Acts as well as assure National Environmental Policy was followed. They would also have to rate the EIS on a scale acceptable or unacceptable. With Ecology having predicted air quality violations and the CASE group's water specialist having sued for over 100 violations of the clean water act in the past year, it was unlikely EPA could approve this project. The Governor would then have to certify the project's compliance with all known environmental laws. We all thought it would be easier for the Governor to certify their breaking them all!

Now, how in the world would it be possible to do all this when everything in the EIS pointed out one, two, three, ten violations of law maybe 50 for water, air, soil, wetlands, human health, historical properties effects, road damage, fugitive dust, mining, barging through endangered grass beds, noise pollution and the list goes on. This is one of the biggest, if not the biggest air polluter in the state. There is no doubt it is the biggest producer of noise pollution. The airport can make far more noise disrupting 100,000 people day and night at any hour and all hours without a single recourse you can take besides calling them and asking them to stop, which they ignore. This facility had 18 listed contaminated sites, some critical. They would consider adding more of this type of activity and even consider it to be legal? How can this be?

The airport claimed throughout the EIS that most impacts would be minimized and many existing problems fixed, some would even magically disappear. It often sounded like it would be a brighter and better world if there were just one more runway.

Somehow, the air quality was going to get better with a third runway. I know you must be wondering, like I was, how you can add polluters but have pollution levels go down? Apparently, the runway wasn't to accommodate more aircraft, but the same amount would come with or without the runway and by building another runway, congestion that causes greater amounts of pollution would be reduced. Foggy delays cause congestion because planes can't land safely and efficiently so they become stuck in a holding pattern miles high waiting for the fog to lift before they can land. This creates great pollution problems in the skies around the city even though it is never estimated in the model at this height. On the ground, planes are sitting all over the tarmac, idling, waiting for a gate because gates are full or pilots can't see them through the fog, then you have more pollution. But would it be possible for the same number to come with or without a runway? What was the limit? Nowhere did the document tell us what the limits were. Can unlimited numbers be crammed in? Minnie had a letter from the FAA saying there was a theoretical operational capacity for Sea-Tac at 110 per hour with two runways which would increase to 140 with a third runway. Theoretically you could add this increase to all the figures if they were willing to admit a capacity increase. Then logically, if the whole world doesn't turn upside down while you do calculations, if planes pollute at all, more planes equals more pollution, right? So you would think.

In the draft, I was surprised to see another set of monitoring. I didn't know the Port had tested the air in the terminal and around the curb front because of employee complaints. Officers were complaining about headaches, dizziness, nausea and other ailments indicative of carbon monoxide poisoning. Although the report concluded the levels were below industrial and workplace standards for exposure limits, I suspect the regulation assumed short term high levels, not the constant high levels going on at an airport. To compare with the workplace regulations, all measurements were of a short duration. Airport workers are at risk with exposure to high levels of emissions which certainly will have a long-term cumulative effect.

Short term levels of carbon dioxide measured at 450 to 500 parts per million with a peak of 1394. Carbon monoxide peaked at 147 parts per million (ppm). Nitrogen dioxide peaked at .3 with an average of .1 which is twice as high as the annual federal standard of .053.[28] The only long term sampling was an eight hour average of 10 parts per million of carbon monoxide which was detected at the Delta Departure gate on November 27 1991.[29] The eight hour standard is 9 ppm.

Even though the narrative suggested everything was fine because levels were below workplace standards, the public is present at the airport, and people with sensitivities, the elderly and children are being exposed. But these alarming findings did not attract the attention of regulators as they should.

Results of another testing for soot were in this section of the EIS where samples were taken from a clothesline, deck and gutter at three residences, only one of which is in the flight path. Only the test in the flight path detected high levels of pyrene, a highly carcinogenic polycyclic aromatic hydrocarbon (PAH) reported to be present in jet exhaust.[30] For some reason, the narrative attached to the analysis which included the high level of pyrene, failed to note its presence.

Airports and FAA typically report fungus, ambiguous and undefined debris, insect parts and other nondescript generalizations in their tests for soot. What needed to happen after collection is for the so called 'debris' to be chemically tested to determine the exact rate and chemical composition of the assorted material collected. In the EIS, one such unscientific and indiscernible analysis using a 'swab' measuring milligrams of debris that nobody understands in terms of parts per million, reported spider web. Who cares? I want to know what kind of analysis found the spider web. Did they eyeball this whole thing or did they actually run the web through a machine? The report concludes:

> "...the clothesline sample, was dark gray and contained a significant population of cellular fragments from a common black fungal species. It also contained natural minerals, organic soil particles, and some soot. The soot was a(sic) very low levels compared to the other materials present. The soot could have come from a variety of sources, road traffic exhaust, fireplaces, incinerators, etc. and does not indicate **only** jet engine exhaust. (emphasis added)

> ...the wood deck/gutter sample, was a medium gray in color and contained natural minerals as the dominant particle type. Tire wear, charred wood, cenospheres, weld spheres, black slag, fungal material, rust, magnetite, **soot** and some insect parts were the black particles in the sample.(emphasis added) Other particles included an off-white spray paint, glass fiber, pollens, plant parts, spider web, etc.
> Note: This residence is the only one of the three located in the flight path and where pyrene was detected. There are no main roads near this residence. It is isolated on a private road and the second floor deck where pyrene was found

backs up to a large wooded area several blocks wide. The only source of any pollution near this deck are low flying overhead jets.)

Lastly;

> ...the sample from the rafters, was a light gray in color and was dominated by paint particles. Mixed with the paint were a number of larger black particles. These particles were not *fine soot* but larger particles inconsistent with the jet exhaust particles. These larger particles were a pyrolytic carbon more typical of a fireplace or open burning of wood. (emphasis added)

The study concluded:

> The clothesline sample was black because of the presence of a black fungal growth. The deck/gutter sample was dark because of light scatter caused by the small particles and the presence of a number of light absorbing particles, including natural minerals, industrial debris, road wear, traffic (truck, bus and car) exhaust, and fireplace debris. The rafter sample included some black particles that were much to(sic) large to be from any jet engine. Their source was more consistent with fireplace smoke and tire wear."[31]

Hard to imagine how that road wear, what the authors assert is the likely source for the petroleum based soot, leaped off the road, traveled two blocks, went around the house, and then traveled upward 12 feet landing onto the top of the deck. Amazing. I can understand how the spider web got there, the spider brought it. I don't know what intricate scientific testing found the spider web but I don't discount that it was there.

The large soot from the rafter was dismissed because of size. Ecology said soot from jet engine combustion called particulate is

mostly fine. Doesn't say ALL. Interesting how the authors didn't even carry over the word soot when they said; these particles are <u>not</u> fine soot but larger particles, (not soot?). Then what? Is it larger insect particles, larger nuclear fallout? How about larger soot? How much larger? There is soot in every sample. Also interesting how they say "soot was a (they meant to say at) very low levels compared to the other materials present". It looks like they start to panic at even writing the word soot and back up by saying it could have come from a variety of sources and name a bunch. Then at the end they say it does not indicate <u>only</u> jet engine exhaust. Doesn't this imply some of it <u>is</u> jet engine exhaust? Then we need to know if it contains PAH. It doesn't take much PAH to cause cancer, otherwise the state limit wouldn't be set so low.

I called the EPA. I had already contacted some people at the air quality section of the region X office when I was working on writing my little report on the MFG air quality sampling preliminary survey. I was put in touch with someone new I hadn't talked to yet named Jim*[1] who seemed very friendly and caring. It was a little different talking to him than it had been talking to Ecology and PSCAA. Everyone I had talked to at these two agencies made it perfectly clear right from the get-go that they could not and would not be able to do anything about the emissions at Sea-Tac. It didn't seem right to me that I was caring more about the environment than the environmental protection agencies the public pays to do that job. They just didn't seem to have a heart. But Jim seemed different. I started talking about the EIS and he said he had looked at it but didn't know where to start since it was so big. I was ready to help with that and I asked him to turn to a few pages I had looked at which said added polluters equals less pollution. I also said look at those inventory numbers. Thousands of tons of emissions in our neighborhoods! Isn't that unreal?

---

[1] Denotes name change for people I have not contacted for permission to use their names in my book.

I asked him to look at the ridiculous automobile produced carbon monoxide (CO). Wow! He was surprised at that amount. I knew it was wrong. It was way too high I was getting ready to explain why it was completely wrong, either a purposeful manipulation or a ridiculous mistake. Ecology's report for Sea-Tac had cars at 502 metric tons per year, planes at 3,121. This EIS had cars at 16,676 tons per year, planes at 1,365. Planes cut in half, cars 30 times higher. I said yeah, isn't that crazy? I knew they must have a reason to hide the real information about jets. Frankly, it's scary. But the only reason I could think of for why automobile emissions were so high was in case someone monitored the area and wanted to control it, they would surmise it must be the cars and would hopefully avoid looking at the planes. They could have kept it reasonable though or just a little higher than the jets but they blew it out of proportion. At any rate, these figures were wacky and backwards, but Jim seemed concerned and he wanted to look into it. I thought for a minute about making a case for why those figures were completely wrong, but sensing his concern to get involved I let it go. I didn't want to run the risk of not being able to adequately make my case, especially when the agencies were debunking the older studies and calling the new EIS the most comprehensive, fantastic analysis to date! Jim might write me off completely and it would be a disaster. So I said, wow, yes, that is unreal and should be looked into.

I told him the peak hour departure figures from the Emissions and Dispersion Model (EDMS) the consultant used were too small, not worst case but average day level. Ecology had used 72, the present EIS used 43.9. I told Jim that the 1991 Ecology report had 68 tons per year of jet produced particulate but this EIS had only 0.23.

There were other things I was concerned about. Prior to the draft, agencies had written comments on things they wanted included in the air quality section. Margaret Corbin at PSCAA wrote:

"The Chicago study only addressed a limited number of toxic air contaminants, only 30 carcinogens. Please address all toxic air contaminants for which information is reasonably available.

I was surprised at the high estimates of formaldehyde, 1,3-butadiene and polynuclear aromatic hydrocarbons that were emitted from Midway airport. These chemicals have a higher toxicity than benzene and would be of particular concern to our Agency."[32]

Jim said he would look into some of this information and get back to me.

According to FAA's letter, if you have or can have 70 peak hour takeoffs you could have 40 landings occurring at that same time since 110 is possible. Planes still land during peak takeoff hour. I've seen it. Theoretically, you could compare that to 90 takeoffs with 50 landings at the same time for the future build scenario assuming 140 is possible as the FAA letter indicates. Peak takeoff is the requirement of the model since this mode produces the most pollution for worst-case. At this point I had talked myself into believing that if they compared dual simultaneous departures with a third runway, to a peak single stream, the air pollution levels would be significantly higher and this project would appear out of compliance. I was hoping Jim would somehow force the consultant to admit the real purpose and need and to be honest with their calculations of worst-case. Not average day level, not 43.9 not 50.1. No. Maximum for the highest pollution numbers you can get so you know the worst situation that might occur so you can plan mitigation needed to protect public health. What part of the aircraft is that .9 fraction? Is it a flap? Does it pollute? What is that fraction doing there?

Even though Jim seemed really nice, I was so afraid of coming across like a kook. I knew I didn't have anybody who could understand what I was talking about outside of a few engineers and doctors in our CASE group or at the agencies. I was arguing with the regulators at PSCAA and Ecology most of the time. PSCAA insisted we should rely on the calculations in the current EIS. Ecology assured me their 1991 study was only a preliminary screening and they didn't do as careful a job as they were sure the current consultants working for the Port had done. I was alone in my attempt to make them aware the current EIS was a load of crap. Ecology had nothing to gain or lose from their outcome, the EIS consultants did. Independent studies raised the level of concern while the Port's EIS dispelled them all.

Up until now, I didn't care who I alienated. I felt the regulators I was talking to were either bought off or didn't care so I pushed. My ideas were met with such hostile resistance I knew if I pushed too hard with Jim it might be a mistake. I didn't want this to happen. We needed an ally. I had to be careful. I had to be patient.

I mailed the copy of the FAA capacity letter to Jim along with some bullet points of things I thought were important. I also sent a copy of an article from airport tower personnel talking about 59 takeoffs in 20 minutes, 75 leaving in the morning rush in summer.[33] I had read through the National Environmental Policy Act (NEPA) and found that the Port and FAA as co-authors of the EIS were federally required to add together ALL reasonably foreseeable impacts of projects considered part of the overall development. This meant that if they had any jet produced particulate, which they had forgotten to estimate, they would have to add it to the haul truck particulate and find out what the total worst case effect might be to the local environment and people living nearby. All projects, and there were many, would have to be considered cumulatively, not separately as was the plan by the authors of the EIS. They maintained in their narrative they had no idea what other projects, still in the planning stage, were going to produce. Jim maintained they had to add them up. So I sent him a list of all the planned projects I knew about.

Figures used for air pollution calculations came from the consultant's use of the FAA's standard airport model and I wanted to get a hold of it and look at what assumptions were used. I called the FAA and the lead expert on the EIS offered to sell it to me for $250.00. I couldn't spare that much so I asked the ACC who had funding from a utility tax collection to fight the expansion. FAA was willing to sell it to the ACC for a cut rate price of $200.00, but ACC declined the offer. Seems they had their own team of experts working on the EIS through their attorneys they had hired to fight expansion. They were working on the purpose and need, foggy delays, noise and land use. ACC felt that air would be a lot of work and they might not have time to add it to their already full plate of issues. I was so disappointed in the ACC's unwillingness to assist me, especially when we were all in the same battle and I was willing to volunteer my time to muddle through the input, whatever it turned out to be. This would not be the last time I would beg the ACC for help and be disappointed by their response.

CONFORMITY

Before the ACC had hired their current legal team they had a local firm give them advice on what issues to pursue to legally challenge and even stop the runway project. Minnie had given me a copy of their memorandum addressed to RCAA and up until this time I had not understood it at all. But now, all of a sudden it made sense to me, maybe because the Port's consultant had tried so hard to create a mythical zero increase in emissions with the project which forced me to want to find out why they had done that. Conformity with the Clean Air Act (CAA) is a requirement that federal projects not cause a new violation of any air quality standard, make an existing violation worse or delay attainment of any standard. The EIS admitted several violations of the federal standard.

Since federal and state transportation improvement program (TIP) funding is related to attainment of the NAAQS, violations at the airport could become priorities for mitigation. Regionally, these might move them to the top of the list since their problems could create funding deficiencies. It wouldn't be the Port who would pay for their roadway improvements through our tax dollars or their own revenues, it would be us through a much larger federal pot through PSRC. This was possibly the reason for the ridiculously high rates from the automobile inventory. This is a double edged sword, while part of the transportation improvement program funding might aid their overall development, conformity might kill the project altogether.

Because ozone is not estimated in most models but is a result of other emissions added together, nitrogen oxides and hydrocarbons combined with heat/sunlight, attached to the conformity approval is a requirement for a limit on the tons per year a project can produce called de-minimus thresholds. In our area of nonattainment the limit was 100 tons of nitrogen oxides and hydrocarbons. I had recalculated emission totals considering the theoretical increases from Minnie's FAA letter finding violations of de-minimus thresholds. In other areas of the country, like Chicago, where the nonattainment status is severe, the limit might be as low as 10 tons or even zero.

Using an average figure that I derived from all the operations, I found that an addition of as few as 14,000 jets would add more than 100 tons of NOx. Adding 30 movements an hour, a possibility according to the FAA letter, could exceed the yearly total with-project allowed limit in a month.

The EIS admitted nitrogen dioxide and carbon monoxide might violate the federal standard. They hadn't predicted any problems with particulate, but I had guessed that the digging, hauling and dumping of 27 million cubic yards of fill dirt for the runway plateau might cause a little dust. Particulate violations had already been discussed by Ecology for the jets by themselves. But not only was the jet particulate set far too low, there were unusually low estimates for the haul truck trips. I thought it was strange that shortly after Ecology had predicted potential violations of the particulate federal standard from jets and EPA's Midway analysis had such a high amount, the EDMS model was altered so dramatically. Was this coincidence or malicious?

Jim seemed to understand the conformity issue and what it meant for the EIS approval process when I next talked to him. I believed I had found a great tool to use which could effectively kill the project, but I couldn't get anybody in the CASE group to support it. Nobody understood what I was talking about except one member who began a campaign to halt EPA involvement. She was sure the same Port manipulations of law that had taken away the communities civil rights also preempted EPA from getting involved to protect our environment. I just about had a heart attack when I found out she had been talking to Jim about this. Even though I thought she was philosophically correct in her assertion, I asked her to please stop. EPA believed they should be involved. Why try to convince them otherwise? Many activists have their own area of expertise and people are very passionate because they are being personally injured. I don't blame anyone for not supporting my own issue. However, in her zeal to make people understand the unconstitutional make-up of the Port of Seattle she nearly innocently and unknowingly destroyed my only hope. Jim had disregarded her claims. He told me he thought her ideas were a little unusual. Apparently he was unfamiliar with government abusing people they represent. He was absolutely an optimist, what I call a cup half full guy. I had a dozen conspiracy theories dripping from my pen daily, but it would have been difficult to convince him that anyone had anything but the best intentions. If the Port hadn't done a thorough job at least they were trying. If the consultants erred, it was probably an innocent mistake they would gladly correct.

Jim also told me he had contacted the consultant about the peak hour figure of 43.9 and they told him the model would automatically double it to 87.8 for total takeoffs and landings. I said I think they're lying. It didn't make sense to me that the same model now using 87 would have results almost cut in half from Ecology's use of 72.

There was far too big a difference in the number for it to be a simple mistake either. One or the other was completely wrong. He said he would try to find out if the model automatically defaults to double that number. But he made a point to tell me the consultant was very persuasive that only 43 planes could take off in a peak hour and no more because of constraints on contrail separation between departing planes. This didn't agree with FAA's letter to Minnie admitting 110, Ecology's number and a newspaper article. Something was terribly wrong or I was misinterpreting things I didn't yet understand. This is one of the tangles that had to be unraveled and because so many unknowns were involved, it would be difficult to find the best knot to untie first. Are landings and takeoffs estimated together for pollution totals in the model or just takeoffs? Had Ecology misused the assumptions? Who knows…I was unsure where the problem was but I was sure there was one.

Nearly every time I called Jim he would take the consultants side. He would patiently explain to me how they professionally and correctly calculated their data and each time I would rip it apart. They must have been visiting his office daily. It was becoming a vocation for me to bring Jim back out of the fog the consultants were creating. The consultants seemed very clever in the way they confused and manipulated the information, which I certainly believed was practiced. I guess Jim had about enough so he made a bold move. He wanted to know who was right. I am still amazed he would even consider doing what he did with such a crowd of experienced, professional consultants visiting his office to compare with the word of one homemaker making wild claims over the phone from little or no experience whatsoever.

He went to the airport and was allowed to sit unaccompanied in the tower with the staff. Shooting the breeze he asked them how many planes they thought they could push out in a peak hour and they told him 65, easy. They also told him that during that period, there are landing aircraft as well, but peak times for takeoffs and landings differ throughout the day. They alternate the two runways for both or either depending on demand. Still, in the end he learned a lot from this single experience and I assured him I believed the model must default the rest from the peak figure. Jim believed in worst-case and he wanted to see a real world bad situation, not an average day/week level the consultants had provided. I was surprised to learn he was the lead at EPA on the EIS process and that he would be responsible for approving or not approving the project as written. These many weeks I had been talking to him, I didn't know this. It was a great day when he called and told me he had been in the tower. He now knew 65 was possible so when the consultants told him no more than 43 because of contrail separation, he now knew someone had been lying.

But not knowing what EPA would do or say, I had to quickly put together my own comments so I questioned the numbers, the data input, the conclusions and mostly the result of no increased pollution with more polluters. I created nice tables of figures showing how the numbers of jets in different scenarios would cause a violation of the conformity rule for de-minimus thresholds exceeded for ozone precursors. I said the project is illegal, it cannot be funded, supported or approved by the FAA with the predicted violations. I asked my brains out in every way I thought would be important. I made a list of cumulative projects, cited the rule in NEPA for the sponsor to add them all together, the problems that would be involved with the governor certifying the project, etc. I had never done anything like this before and although I didn't know what happens next, I had very high hopes that once someone looked at this reasonable sounding rebuttal to this gigantic project with such huge impacts, how could it be approved? Jim asked me for a copy of my comments and I was flattered. At this time in history, few of my friends had personal computers, nobody had a fax machine or copier. I had to print out an extra copy of everything and mail it to EPA and I copied everyone from the local cities to the governor. Paper, envelopes, extra postage was coming out of an extremely tight family budget.

Minnie and her group had put together a book covering the history of the cities which would be affected by the project. Contributors to the book added pictures and details of the area that dated back to the late 1800's. Audrey and others put together a history of the local school district which dated back to 1882. Minnie had citied many laws which were being broken by the Port, pointed out problems in their financial accounting, etc. Rose had included lists of people who had lived near the airport and died of cancer. One neighborhood had even been bought out by the Port because, Rose and Audrey believed, too many who had lived there had died from brain tumors.

In the backdrop of the whole EIS comment period, there were hearings held by the Port to gather public comments. Many of the CASE members attended meetings and shared their horror stories of being awakened constantly by jet noise, engine testing run-ups, talked about kerosene odors in their neighborhoods. A teacher talked about children on the play-ground crouching and holding their ears as departing jets roared overhead. Out of dozens who spoke against the runway, there were a few people who came to these hearings who spoke in favor. We would always look at the list afterward to see where these people lived. Nearly everyone who spoke favorably lived out of the area.

If anything can be gathered from the so called 'public process', it was that people, agencies, politicians, communities, cities, schools, were overwhelmingly against expansion The only thing that can be favorably said of the public process, which the Port and FAA would later claim was extensive, was that there was one. But it wasn't for the public. It was for the industry to fulfill another obligation. The only option communities had to protest the process was to not go. But if they don't go, someone will show up to say its good and the process is still fulfilled.

When I spoke I said what everyone else said, we are suffering. I asked how they can justify harming 100,000 people with constant noise, emissions, property value losses, children unable to hear in their schools, is it right to do this to people? Especially just so you can have less delay from fog which is an unproven problem at Sea-Tac? One representative from a district far away from the airport came up to me after one of these meetings and reminded me that I benefited because I lived near the airport. I asked him how that can be since I only perceived harm? He said our communities receive an economic benefit because each traveler getting off a plane might stop at one of our local stores to shop. Other communities don't have the same benefits. I asked; what would they buy? We have homes and grocery stores because we are a neighborhood. Do we get someone from New Jersey stopping to buy some gum before heading over to his hotel in a different city since we had none in ours? What if the cab driver has gum? Does he then go straight to the hotel without stopping to shop in our neighborhood? I doubt very much people are going to do any serious grocery shopping or use a local car repair once they land here on a plane. Does billions in losses, our health problems, our kids being subjected to less than a standard education because of constant noise disruption, jet fumes, prostitution, jet ghetto and transient population seem better somehow because some foreign visitor buys gum here? Was this guy crazy or something? He had just listened to dozens of people talking about the horrors of living here. How would he like an airport in his neighborhood? Fact is, nobody wants one, and for good reason. I wouldn't wish it on anyone except this guy. It is terrible to awake at 4:00 a.m. to the loud rumble of the 20 year old Fed Ex DC 10 groaning over your house and know each day that it never ever stops.

The home insulation might make the inside of your house a little quieter, but you can't have a conversation outside. You can't use your own yard for anything. It is a war zone. Kids can't play happily outside. When my son played baseball at Sunset Field, you couldn't even hear the crack of the bat hitting the ball when a plane went over. Our children have to yell at their playmates for them to hear each other every 30 seconds as planes scream overhead. This is a terrible way to live and nobody should have to live like this all day and all night every day just so someone from far away can come to our town to buy gum and go home to their cozy quiet house. How dare he tell me I should be happy because someone is going to buy gum in my neighborhood. He would never trade homes with me, never. His solution if I am unhappy? Sell my home and move away. But who is going to buy it? Now that I know how bad it is, how can I in good conscience sell it to someone without first making them aware of the risks?

This is the reason why the Port wants so badly for everyone to believe that we moved here so it is our fault. They can be absolved from responsibility while creating classes of people, ones who are smart who would never buy a house near an airport and ones who are dumb who would. When our citizens commented on the EIS, we showed how some of our school buildings pre-date even the invention of flying. Our school district was the most heavily populated district in the state when the airport was still a farm. Most of our neighborhoods were here before jets started flying in commercial service regularly in the 1960's. Yes, I am one who moved in later, but the planes, nonetheless, moved into me in 1989 with the four-post plan. I didn't ask to have my property sooted by jets which, according to the Port, didn't exist while according to others was going to kill me and my family. I think it would only be fair to say it is our fault, if they were forthcoming with the truth. The truth isn't a pretty picture and I know why they want to hide it.

ASNA in 1979 required them to remove not insulate non-compatible land uses, draw maps and most definitely should have prompted guidelines that builders of single family residential properties stay away. In a sense the FAA has taken seriously the intent of ASNA since in their building of Denver International (DIA) they created a 64,000 acre buffer around it. Dallas Fort Worth has 18,000 acres behind a fence with a noise mitigation program outside that fence line. Our entire mitigation area is less acreage than half the size of DFW! It was the Port who knew what they were going to do to us, not us who knew. The onus was on them to prepare and plan, not us. There were no signs posted in my neighborhood saying "Don't move here or you will be sorry." There should have been. In 1980 when I moved in, there were 230 daily takeoffs and most didn't go over my house. They took off and quickly turned toward their destination. This was called a scatter pattern. Many were disturbed a few times a day. But in 1994, just before the EIS process really got going, there were now 550 takeoffs per day directly over my house. Now some were disturbed many times per day. All they were going to offer me for this horrible inconvenience was some insulation. They had already taken our investment and quality of life, maybe even our health but still wanted even more. I would have to waive all my rights to obtain insulation which had no guarantees to work, no guarantees for the work, and no recourse for me if it didn't work.

Now with the EIS, and the so called 'extensive' public process, the Port had yet another opportunity to warn people about the terrible consequences of their operations on human health and the environment. They could have said the jet emissions are dangerous. They could have offered to spend their resources on getting people out of the danger zone rather than buying dirt or spending it on propaganda pieces proclaiming their humanitarian efforts to help the idiots.

Hundreds of people ended up commenting on the EIS. Many were just one or two pages of concerns. Others were nearly books from citizen groups near the airport and many miles away. Environmental justice came up from Rainier Valley citizens who had claimed the landing and takeoff pattern had been routed over their low-income families in the months preceding the EIS release. A Boeing engineer wrote over 100 pages of comments concerned about property value losses and salability issues with Normandy Park homes. She had tables and lists of trends in property value showing while property values in Seattle were rising Normandy Park homes, one of the nicest neighborhoods near the airport, had began to actually drop once the plans for the third runway were announced. She also noted several engineering issues with the third runway embankment, fill, wall as well as water and endangered species concerns. Working ten hour days while raising a family and finding time to research and put together this document in 30 days is a giant task that has gone largely unrecognized. She is an expert whose concerns were from an educated and experiential background on issues directly relating to the proposed construction. Yet her concerns as well as the aviation delay expert hired by the cities to dispel the foggy figures garnered no more respect or response than the individual who cited noise disturbance.

FAA is required by NEPA to provide reasons and rule of law to indicate why the comment(s) do not warrant further consideration, besides their own rules that exempt them from nearly everything. No specific laws were cited which excused them from many illegalities cited in comments. Comment noted was a popular response. Insulation, buy-outs, national leader in dollars spent was cited for people whose lives were in ruin from noise. No worse than other urban areas was the response to numerous complaints of illness, cancers and deaths in the communities. Nobody was on board to make them properly respond, or for that matter, properly anything, except for one little problem, EPA.

Chapter 8

FINAL EIS

The document now included our comments, their responses and a few additional pages of data and narrative just as confusing as the draft. EPA had sent me a copy of their department's comments. I was jumping up and down for joy when I read their rating of the EIS, EO-2, environmental objections-lack of data. EPA asked questions about the peak departure figures, cumulative impact analysis, haul-truck dust and most importantly to me, the need for the Port to conduct an almost never before heard of, draft conformity analysis which included a description of mitigation for known air quality violations.

I was so excited I could hardly stand it. I knew, although I had not received confirmation from anyone on this yet, that you cannot mitigate nitrogen dioxide violations from jet takeoffs unless you reduce takeoffs. If EPA pushed them to increase the peak hour takeoffs, these violations would be much worse than the draft had predicted. EPA's comments had echoed my every concern and they had understood and properly applied the conformity rule. But where were their comments about noise, water quality, endangered species habitat being ripped away, historical properties, wetlands and all the other environmental problems? I called Jim and asked him. He said that early on in the process they had to make a decision where to focus their attention and decided to pick air quality. I asked him why they would pick air when they had a plethora of issues including the most popular one; noise? He said it was because I had called. What about the hundreds of people who had been concerned about all these other issues? Noise has always been the biggest issue with airports. How about the cities and their attorneys? Jim said no one else had called. Even though nobody contacted EPA besides me, the news about their comments quickly spread through the communities and pretty soon, everyone had a copy, including the ACC attorneys.

Now that the comment period was over and FAA, who expected the final EIS to be the last word from the agencies before proceeding to a build-out, had offered to sell me the EDMS model input for a discounted price of $13.00. I thought the EIS would be short, concise and to the point, maybe a few hundred pages. Similarly I thought the model input would be similar to Ecology's 1991 readout, about 10 pages of data. Instead, I received the model in the mail in the form of 13 floppy discs. Just one of these was too large for my old computer and I couldn't even open it, let alone the model to run it on. I asked for help from a friend who was working for Microsoft. He was surprised by the amount of data. After about a week he asked me to be specific about what I wanted within the thousands of pages of data he was looking at. I asked him for emission rates, taxi, takeoff and idling times, type of aircraft and tons per year totals.

Taxi times to and from the third runway were the same as those from the first and second. EPA has recommendations for time in mode for congested airports at 26 minutes which includes taxiing in and out, idling and waiting for departure they call queue. This consultant had used 8 minutes for medium jets to 15 minutes for large for all modes on all runways. The Port was adding nearly one half mile to the taxi distance with a third runway with zero increase in time which would mean zero increase in emissions especially carbon monoxide.

The engineer in the CASE group had questioned whether fractional numbers such as 43.9 departures eliminated or fractioned an engine or plane and produced goofy results. I couldn't tell from the data I was looking at if this were true or not, but I did notice that all particulate for every jet aircraft was set at zero. EPA and Ecology reports both included particulate at 50 to 60 tons per year. What happened to all the jet particulate? I sent a letter to the FAA and after a few weeks got a response saying particulate had been eliminated because it was found to be inaccurate. Was zero more accurate? His letter said particulate was still estimated as smoke number when new aircraft engines were tested and certified. The Federal Aircraft Engine Emission Database (FAEED) contains the new aircraft engine emission facts and according to FAA, the consultant could have altered the zero defaults with data from FAEED. I also now learned that the modeling included all new engine factors, not the thousands of older, dirtier engines operating in our neighborhoods meaning the real world factors were probably much worse than the modeling.

I heard from EPA that the consultants felt it was too time consuming to try and estimate particulate from jets. Whose time? Aren't they being paid to do the job? Wouldn't taking more time be financially beneficial for them? Ecology told me that in 1991 it was difficult to use the data since smoke number which is what FAEED reports, must be converted to particulate. Ecology did it and so did EPA in the 1993 Midway report. Their numbers are relatively similar although the two were completely unrelated in time and authorship. So apparently it is possible. Apparently, the EIS isn't the most comprehensive. I tried to make a case for the inaccuracies without any success.

The EIS claimed there would be no way to predict dust from hauling of the 25 or so million cubic yards of fill dirt because a contractor had not been chosen and haul routes were still undecided. EPA had asked for an estimate anyway. I had commented that the jet particulate when added to the haul particulate would cause a particulate problem that would exceed 100 tons per year in the air-shed. Of course, I was considering the jets produced some. The final EIS included no further discussion of this than the EIS had contained. Haul truck emissions, even though 57 double haul trucks an hour were considered, were negligible in the analysis, less polluting than cars. Local air quality officials told me the particulate was of no concern to them because we were not in a particulate non-attainment zone. What about violations of the standard? Jets by themselves were expected to cause a violation. If this data were calculated and added to haul truck emissions, added to digging, hauling and dumping, maybe even added to the dozen other projects, surely there would be trouble.

The engineer had calculated that the amount of dirt being hauled was equal to one wheelbarrow full for every single citizen living in King County or an amount equal to an 18 inch square reaching to the moon. If this project didn't cause a fugitive dust or particulate problem, what would? The regulators didn't seem to care.

I don't understand either why someone didn't force them to choose a nearby borrow pit and pick a route in fact use them all. It's only modeling where we pretend with simulations. There are only three roads into the third runway area. They would need them all! And they would use them all plus they built a couple more roads besides. Couldn't someone see they were stalling? Couldn't anyone tell they were hiding something?

EPA had asked for a cumulative analysis and FAA and Port responses were nearly the same as the EIS, with statements like; until project specific plans can be finalized, a cumulative impact analysis is not possible at this time. While the FAA and Port later insisted they had done it, I said it's not there. One of my letters letting Jim know they hadn't complied with EPA requests was forwarded to the head of Region X EPA, who wrote back in defense of the consultant that they had completed it and referenced the sections the consultant claimed contained the details. I searched every section, found the sentence or two in each area of environmental impact where the FAA and Port had said 9 times out of 10 that they couldn't do it and sent it back to the EPA. I didn't hear any more about it. Apparently, on this issue, EPA had accepted FAA and the Port's word they had done it, rather than searching the 10,000 pages of data themselves. It was *never* actually done. But at this point in time, I had so many irons in the fire; I didn't have the time to follow through with debating back and forth. This would be one of many times the agencies would falsely claim it had been completed with reference to previous analysis as per the consultant's word.

EPA had also asked for a draft conformity analysis. The final EIS said they didn't have to do it. They thought they were exempted from it for three reasons. First, the carbon monoxide violations were not their fault. All these cars were coming to the airport and they had no control over it. Maybe they figured all those cars would come whether they had an airport there or not since we have great gum out here. Second, the nitrogen dioxide violation at a receptor on airport property would not expose the public so they didn't need to worry about it. Lastly, they maintained if they were to do a conformity analysis for tons per year, and existing violations of the NAAQS, their project would conform so they didn't need to. EPA disagreed.

There were internal letters sent back and forth between the attorney for the FAA and EPA asking what to do. I didn't know about these letters until after everything was over, but it appears that FAA was trying to find a way around the conformity problems. They asked EPA if they, for instance, dropped the terminal from the plan, and decided it had separate utility (pretended is more like it), could they conform for carbon monoxide? EPA answered with an affirmative but they would still have to mitigate for the terminal drives and International Boulevard with additional dedicated turn lanes or whatever it might take to reduce emissions. Of course, all these discussions were based upon that ridiculous, mythical 16 thousand tons of CO from cars. I thought it was funny though when Jim told me mitigation might mean the Port would have to buy up all the old cars in Sea-Tac City. I also thought it was risky since I knew the Port with their large tax collection ability could afford just about anything and raising the cost of the project would not be a deterrent.

The predicted nitrogen dioxide violation was another problem. EPA did not agree that an area without public exposure was any less important than an area of exposure because the law didn't differentiate. A violation of the federal standard was a violation, period. Unless mitigated the project could not be approved or supported. But the argument between the agencies did not focus on the problem of how impossible it would be to mitigate nitrogen dioxide which is produced primarily as a result of jet takeoffs. I knew it would be impossible to mitigate unless there were less jets, less jet engines or less takeoffs. That was not about to ever be considered an option especially when the real plan behind the foggy delays boloney was to increase operations. Nobody I was talking to wanted to talk about how to mitigate this violation. The predicted spot where the violation occurred wasn't even the highest in the grid. It had been chosen arbitrarily as a single violation where, in actuality, there were a dozen higher ones that were ignored. I couldn't get anyone to recognize this gross oversight and nobody was reading the analysis. Granted, it was more boring than watching snails race, but these guys are the experts, not me. They should be accustomed to looking at boring data stuff and better at it than I was. Maybe there was more going on. I will probably never know.

Jim was saying that approval could be conditional based upon a monitoring agreement. If monitoring the air with actual credible equipment for a long enough period would either prove or disprove the existence of these violations then they could proceed to a final conditional approval. This seemed to me like a cop-out. I wanted more. I wanted the EPA to deny approval based upon falsified data, missing data, irresponsible data and too many impacts. I wanted everyone to recognize there was no real world worst case involved anywhere in the consultant's analysis. I wanted to go even further than that. I wanted them to admit they were lying.

Meanwhile, the cities had made quite a good case against the foggy assumptions. Many professionals had commented extensively on noise. Experts on water had exerted great talent and insight on the potential problems with the project and even the existing airport violating the Clean Water Act. The inadequacy of the existing Industrial Wastewater System (IWS) to handle the additional load, and contaminated areas in the airport operations area (AOA) were cited. Other professional experts and citizens had commented.

EPA's comments were very similar to mine, no accident. They got their ideas on conformity from me and I got mine from a very smart environmental lawyer. But my much harsher questions with far less wiggle room than EPA's, were rolled into innocuous responses to EPA. Few people knew that I had been working on EPA daily and had spent thousands of man-hours educating myself beforehand. Without EPA though, my concerns would have been ignored. With EPA on our side these issues had clout. But I would have little control over upper level discussions in Jim's office with the Port and FAA attempting to make an end run around the rules by creating compromises.

Jim wanted the Port to monitor air toxics. I couldn't understand how we could use this information. If violations of the ASIL from the MFG couldn't be legally applied to Sea-Tac since it's not a smokestack, how would a longer term study be applied? Even if it were a better study, there was already a better study from Midway backed by EPA that I couldn't find a way to apply to Sea-Tac. How would a better one at Sea-Tac be used to benefit the communities or stop expansion? Any million dollar air toxics analysis, in my opinion, would need a risk analysis along with epidemiology. I suggested the money could better be spent on monitoring carbon monoxide, nitrogen dioxide and particulates. These all had strong federal rules attached to them that could be used against this expansion program and independent reports indicated as well as the current EIS that there were violations. If they were to find just one nitrogen dioxide or carbon monoxide violation, this would delay the project, delay regional attainment and set back regional transportation plans. This seemed like a much more worthwhile endeavor than spending millions on a three pronged air toxics analysis that might be stalled after the first week for lack of funds.

Haul trucks also produce nitrogen oxides and with hundreds of these in our neighborhoods daily for years, how could it be compliant? Jim was going to try to secure funding and a commitment from the Port for monitoring of CO, NOx and particulate.

PSCAA had also commented and had asked for a risk analysis from air toxics. They had expressed concern about the high rates of emissions in the Midway study and were concerned about the potential cancer risks to nearby communities. The draft EIS discussed the Midway report and mistakenly claimed:

"This study finds that the major contributor to risk is the road vehicles in the study area."[34]

PSCAA also brought up PAH known to be in jet emissions. The final EIS did not have a risk analysis because, the consultant claimed, not enough information was available to conduct one. PAH was not discussed and air toxics were estimated at rates below those previously monitored by MFG. The conclusion again, without defining anything was; 'we are no worse than other urban areas.'

The final EIS however, would normally be the final word from the agency on impacts and expected mitigation efforts, and according to people in control of things like this, would proceed to the Record of Decision (ROD) without as much as a hiccup. But FAA and the Port had failed to complete the conformity analysis and did not increase the peak hour departure figure or list cumulative effects as EPA had requested. So instead of proceeding to the ROD, something new happened. EPA did not approve the EIS and required a first ever Supplemental Environmental Impact Statement (SEIS) be written which would include a draft conformity determination, haul truck estimates and higher peak departure figures. I would now have the opportunity to bring up the missing particulate, the taxi time in mode and the consultants misdeeds in handling responses to my original comments.

Ecology had missed commenting the first time around, but now they could comment on conformity if they desired. Whoever commented on issues carried over into the supplemental would be able to comment further. It was like starting all over with fewer issues.

As many kept reminding me, after this we would have the ACC attorneys who, even though normally representing airports against communities like ours, would sue the FAA and Port over anything they thought winnable. After this, and many of us were sure it would never get this far, the Governor would have to certify the project for air and water quality. How would that be possible? Then the Army Corps would have to permit the wetland destruction with its sure to fail unusual mitigation plan. One process or another was sure to kill it. Upcoming endangered salmon listings might halt the relocation of Miller Creek, a necessary component of the project, as the stream, home to several species about to be listed, was in the way of the runway embankment. If the FAA and Port had been confident they could author and approve their own project without anyone getting in their way, they had been mistaken. If the Port had the FAA co-author the EIS to shelter themselves from trouble on the local or state level, they now had more than their share on the federal level due completely to the federal conformity rule.

I went to city hall in Des Moines during this period between the final EIS and SEIS and some of the staff there, including the representative for ACC, city manager and a councilmember held up their hands in a high five to me and said good work on the conformity issue. This surprised me because up until this time I had not realized anyone besides Jim at EPA had been paying attention to anything I was doing. Most people in our CASE group were off on their own tangent. Everyone believed their issue was the most important. They all were important. But there are so many, from the obvious noise, to the ambiguous soot the Port claims is from nearby traffic, fireplaces or flying saucers, anything but the obvious overhead jets. It is difficult to get one group to fight on one topic. But regardless of the topic of discussion for the group, the Supplement would feature air quality violations and conformity, haul truck dust with cumulative impacts from multiple projects brought to you by Region X EPA,...with honest impacts from peak hour, honest answers to valid questions and a downright inability to build as the anticipated result.

The noise issue has always been the number one national concern for airport sponsors since at least 1979 and is the number one issue with residents. Insulation and buy-outs have been pursued making it difficult, but not impossible for the public to make a case against airports for noise disturbance. However, with the phase out of noisier jets, airports claim noise has been so dramatically reduced, they have no new programs on the drawing board for any further measures that I am aware of. With 25 years or more of planning and manipulations of rule and law on noise issues, it has become very difficult for communities to get anywhere with airports and the FAA on this issue.

Water issues can be a problem for airports because there may be violations of the Clean Water Act with certain discharges airports typically produce, but airports operate and are allowed to discharge under a National Pollution Discharge and Elimination System (NPDES) permit which can pre-empt citing violations on items covered by the permit. As with air, water issues are difficult to prove because it takes testing of the water, a lab to analyze it, an expert to interpret it and a quick follow-up on the possible source of the problem. Since on-airport testing by independent groups or agencies is not normally allowed, tests must be conducted downstream which makes source appointment a topic for debate. Unlike noise however, testing and interpretation can be independent of the industry meaning the outcome cannot be manipulated. Water problems can be more easily observed than toxic air pollution. Air is the most difficult and expensive to analyze, detect and source appoint of the three. But in my mind, if emissions are violating the law and it can be proven it is from jets, you cannot control, mitigate or offset for its effects with insulation or by building a treatment pond. Unlike noise and water, the industry has never had to really deal with a challenge to their emissions. They have been hiding behind its ambiguity with no real plan for defense. What kind of a plan could they possibly develop to curtail jet air pollution when jet operations are predicted to increase and no modification in engines or fuel are on the drawing board?

Shortly after the FAA and Port announced they would be re-writing their EIS with a supplemental an article appeared on the front page of the local paper about forecasts. FAA, concerned about accuracy, had found that more aircraft would come to Sea-Tac in the future so they were re-writing their EIS to reflect these new figures. Was this some kind of joke? FAA concerned about accuracy of numbers of aircraft?

I called Jim at EPA who assured me it was for conformity. He sent me an "Inside EPA" newsletter from their office in Washington DC which discussed the whole situation and the reason behind the re-write:

"The Federal Aviation Administration (FAA), reportedly concerned that an expansion project at the Seattle-Tacoma Airport (Sea-Tac) remains out of compliance with the Clean Air Act's "conformity" provision, has postponed its Record of Decision (ROD) that allows the project to move forward.

The delay comes following months of negotiations between local, state and federal air quality officials seeking an agreement with the FAA and Sea-Tac operator the Port of Seattle that would guarantee no further deterioration of the region's air quality from the proposed Sea-Tac expansion."[35]

Why would they sidetrack with forecasts which, if analyzed, would only make their conformity findings worse? Was it a conspiracy or stupidity? They had already published wild forecasts in years past. Nobody, including them, knew if there would be 440,000 operations by 2010, 460,000 or 472,000. Now they were saying as many as 630,000 could come by 2020. So what? They had no intention of analyzing impacts for this year. The consultants hired by the ACC cities had already proved that the 44% bad weather delay figure was false. Delay figures published by FAA the same year as the final EIS was published, showed Sea-Tac delayed by 1% or less, one of the best on-time records for any airport in the country. The runways purpose and need was based upon a false premise and everyone knew that long before it was proven. Now we had an article showing how someone had gone a little crazy with an excel spreadsheet, but why?

Foggy delays were manufactured, now forecasts. What next?

While working on the air issues, I had learned that my family and I probably were not living in an ideal environment, and although we would lose money on the sale of our home, we needed to get out. Even people at EPA had suggested this was probably my only option.

My two year old dog had died of heart failure. An autopsy had not confirmed the presence of disease or any congenital defect. I used to sit at my table watching him outside on the porch. He loved going outside in the sun. But I wondered if he would be affected and how. I worried about letting him out so much. I often thought of him as a canary in the tunnel. He didn't last long. His untimely death worried me more than my paperwork. Maybe they were not only understating conditions, maybe even the source documents underestimated emissions and it was far worse than Ecology had even calculated.

Once my dog died, I didn't want my children to play outside, since I knew that the walls of my house afforded some small amount of filtration on the emissions and soot. I had also learned from a study of particulates, that the harder you exercise and the deeper you breathe the more likely the fine particulates will go deeper into the lungs and get lodged. The kids wanted to run, ride bikes and play basketball, all of which are vigorous exercise. What kind of a life is this where a mother has to keep kids from playing outside? I didn't want to be over-cautious if I had exaggerated these findings. On the other hand, why take the risk? We lived under the ceiling height where emissions would not disperse. All reports, even the airport

EIS admitted we would experience a ground level impact. It was the extent of the impact that was in dispute, whether the soot were carcinogenic, whether it was landing on our property and how long it might take for the family to develop disease. But if the dog was any indication lasting only two years, it was probably already too late.

My oldest son had told me that a majority of his classmates at school used inhalers and both my sons had bouts with asthmatic symptoms during their childhood. It is no wonder that years later the State would find asthma rates in children in these communities to be 21% higher than average rates in King County. The State would also find hospitalizations for children age 0 to 17 were 51% higher than county rates for pneumonia and influenza..

One night at about 10:00, as I was saying goodnight to my children, I heard a loud thump onto the side of my house. My children were worried about what it might be so I went outside with a flashlight but couldn't see anything.

I had a rose garden on the side of the house where the thump occurred and the next morning, looking up onto the second story I could see that the siding looked damaged and the nails in the corner were half way out. I checked the rest of the house to see if this sort of thing were happening as a matter of wear and didn't see it anywhere else. But what really troubled me were the shiny, metallic looking spots I saw on all my rose bush leaves. Right away I suspected a fuel dumping. Although airports say they only do it in an emergency and only over water, most people who live in flight-paths know it is common for landing jets to dump extra weight since it is dangerous for the landing gear to go in too heavy. Residents have complained of a mist coming from landing planes and news stories have documented such events, including a dumping onto a playground full of children in New Jersey. In 1991 a Port Commissioner, Paige Miller called for plan to relieve neighborhoods of fuel dumped from planes. After hearing alarming comments from residents during an airport expansion hearing she said:

"Person after person came up and said, 'I've given up hanging laundry out because it comes in black,' and 'My doctor asked me if I smoke because in his check of my lungs it looked that way, and I don't (smoke). I just live near the airport,"[36]

But if a landing plane had dumped fuel on my plants, what hit my house? I didn't think liquid wouldn't slam into my siding causing damage and a loud thump. I called Ecology and asked them to come and look at my plants.

About a week later someone showed up and examined the leaves and told me it was a common rose bush problem called black spot. I explained that it had started out as shiny spots but later turned black. She insisted it was a common plant ailment. I didn't believe it. I took some of my leaves to the local nursery and they confirmed what I suspected, that it wasn't black spot at all but something they couldn't identify. I decided to call the FAA and an inspector came over. By this time, I realized the black spots were on every plant in my yard, including leafed trees and flowers in the front garden.

The FAA inspector came a week later and suggested the house thump might have been bathroom waste which sometimes, at high altitudes, freezes onto the plane and once the plane descends, it melts enough to break away. It could fall as a solid chunk which could have caused the damage to the siding and been responsible for the noise, but he didn't think it would be related to the spots on all the foliage. He had no opinion about that, which by now, was eating holes through all the leaves.

I called my homeowners insurance and they said they would pay for a lab test to find out what was on the leaves. Maybe they thought I had damages that could be pinned onto something, although I had no idea whether it was a plane, what plane, what alien spaceship the airport might blame, or maybe my neighbor was smelting metals in an open pit. Who knows why they agreed to cover it. I found a lab near my home and called them, delivered some specimens, and waited for the results.

About a week later they reported the samples had come up with many peaks and some high peaks of what appeared to be hydrocarbons, a component of fuel, and they began trying to find a sample of Jet A fuel for comparison. They had used a gas chromatography analysis. To identify specifically what the compounds were would take a mass spectrometer costing another $1,000 which my homeowners insurance was unwilling to cover and I couldn't spare. Again, the local agencies would not help me.

Although the analysis of Jet A was not an exact match, the lab suggested it was because what had hit my plants was weathered Jet A for which samples were unavailable. They conducted a further analysis of the same type of leaves taken from Mount Rainier forest which did not produce the high hydrocarbon counts or any peaks. The graph was flat. Since I was on a cul-de-sac with little traffic and no wood burning stoves in the area, this left only one real suspect, it had to be over head aircraft. One would assume that if all the spots are on the tops of the leaves all the way up the trees, it had to come from above. All the trees were taller than the top of nearby homes. So I called the FAA back and let them know the results.

Unfortunately, without being able to identify the plane, the airline and the VIN number located on the tail of the plane, there was no way they would do anything. How in the world was I supposed to get the VIN number off the tail of a plane flying over 200 mph at 1,000 feet over my head in the dark let alone being a psychic to know ahead of time that I should be out in the yard at 10:00 p.m. on this particular night with night goggles, a high powered light, a pen and paper, rain gear to protect my skin from fuel and a really tall ladder?

By mid August, all the leaves on trees and plants in my yard had completely disintegrated. The FAA said I could write to the Port and ask to be compensated for my plants. I would have to appeal to a panel of self-appointed community representatives who would consider my request along with hundreds of others which I was certain would be more important. I didn't want more plants. I wanted to be assured it was safe to live in my home. I wanted a normal life.

After reluctantly getting insulated I applied for Transaction Assistance. I had negotiated with the Port's appraiser for months beforehand with my own comparables, proper square feet values and lots of begging. They gave me a better price than I expected but the only offer came from one buyer in three months who was shocked I wouldn't negotiate at least $20,000 off the asking price since it was in a flight path. My real estate agent quit because he felt it was a waste of his time to keep trying to market the house for what was well below replacement cost, but far too high for the area. What is crazy is that we were asking way too much but would have to dramatically downsize if we hoped to buy another house away from the airport. As we struggled through the terribly stressful ordeal of keeping the house in show condition, my husband of 20 years decided he had had enough, enough of all the activism, phone calls, my interference with agencies trying to do their jobs, meetings, my constant research and writing. He wanted a divorce. He gave me back my college fund which was used as the down payment on our first house in West Seattle where we should have stayed, a stipend for my trouble, and I left. So now on top of having to start over analyzing another EIS process, I would have to trade my part-time jobs for full time, move, and reorganize my life. I guess you can't save the world and the marriage at the same time.

I ended up moving into an apartment in Federal Way. It may sound weird, but I chose this place because the plants looked healthy. I had begun to notice the shriveled and withering plants all over in the flight path. Over the years, every mature tree, bush and shrub planted by my neighbors in my old neighborhood has died or withered. There is almost nothing left of the original plants we put in together when everyone first moved there in 1980. Plants thrived for awhile, but in the mid 90's everything started to die. I believed the health of the outdoor plants would be a good indicator of the health of the environment, mostly the air. After several months of living in this new place, my children's asthma cleared up and has never returned but my younger son who was just learning to read in the old neighborhood never completely caught up.

I was hired to work at RCAA with title of Administrative Director.

Chapter 9

SEIS

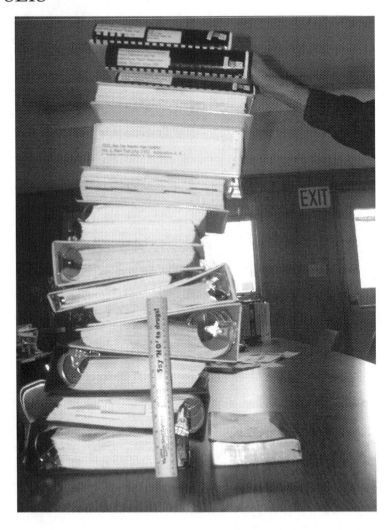

All documents to date, referencing each other, stacked more than three feet in height. EPA was demanding an accumulative impact analysis. Up until this time, the consultants who wrote the EIS were merely mentioning other projects in their analysis. Nothing was being added and I pointed that out to EPA again in between the EIS processes. They continued to ask once again for the dust from hauling to be considered additive. Again, the consultants insisted they couldn't until a contract had been let and haul routes designated. Maybe some contractors are sloppier than others, or some use smaller trucks or teaspoons to do the dumping and they couldn't foresee anything without having details. Needless to say, they had fudged everything else before now, why not write a paragraph saying it might be a little uncomfortable for a few chipmunks while they barge in a small island and who would challenge it?

Jim's request for higher peak hour figures was finally honored. There were now 63 departures considered, but the fleet was altered to nearly half of peak hour takeoffs being light and general aviation aircraft. These produce negligible emissions for NO in comparison to jets. The consultant claimed that jets could not take off close enough together to leave space for contrails to push out 63 in a peak hour. Even though the media and the FAA were asserting this whole extra 2 million dollar re-write was about forecasts, they only raised the air pollution calculations from a maximum of 460,000 2010 annual operations in the final EIS to a new 474,000 an increase of only 14,000 annual polluters. They had never intended to include the pollution for future 525,000 or 630,000 operations. Ecology's fleet mix in 1991 was 70% jets with 70 takeoffs in the peak hour. You would think that the third runway could accommodate more than existing. But we never even got to existing let alone 30 additional as the FAA letter had claimed. Jet particulate was still set at zero.

So they were worried about accuracy. Give me a break.

This time around however, the ACC attorneys were involved with the draft conformity analysis. They had also asserted the data had been manipulated to obtain a positive result. The ACC cities had hired a consultant to analyze the intersection carbon monoxide. I spoke with them several times. They were finding that the cars were probably much worse than the EIS had predicted. Are you kidding me? Within the model they noticed that cars disappeared in the queue between the do-nothing and with-project analyses. I just shook my head in disbelief. From looking at the inventories, it appeared to me the cars had been so overblown, now the consultant was saying it was too low? If this were the plan with the wild carbon monoxide, the Port had certainly succeeded in sidetracking attention away from aircraft emissions. I tried to convince this consultant to get involved in looking at the EDMS data, but they were swamped with the carbon monoxide from cars and didn't have resources to do both.

I was anxious to get Jim involved with the obvious follow-up on his concerns of cumulative analysis and let him know how they had manipulated the results once again. His expertise and background was invaluable to us at this point. He had already spent almost four years on the EIS with scoping comments before the draft EIS, commenting on the draft, final and supplemental, the longest ever for him on an EIS.

But when I called Jim, he wasn't at his desk. I couldn't believe it when I was told he had been taken off the project and transferred to another EPA department. I don't know why this happened, whether it was a result of federal pressure by FAA, attorneys or EPA heads or just the inevitable shuffling within the agency. Maybe he was sick of it or me and asked to be transferred. He wouldn't tell me. I never talked to him again. Shortly after this he would quit the EPA altogether. I consider this a real shame since he was the one person who truly had the environment, health of people and honesty as his focus. He had assured me that no matter how bad it might be one federal agency will not sue another. So he had pushed FAA and the Port as far as he could. The next step, legal action, would have to be up to the ACC attorney's.

The new person who took Jim's place didn't seem interested in the violations, the tons per year, fudging by the consultant, alteration of the fleet mix or anything I brought up. Jim had managed to secure signatures from the Port, its commission, all three air agencies, EPA, Ecology and PSCAA and funding resources for the air quality monitoring program before he left. This would be the primary condition for EPA's approval of conformity, with separate utility on the new terminal to be analyzed in 2010 or thereabouts. His replacement seemed to be content to consider that all reasonable concerns from EPA had now been addressed.

A local news report featured Jim talking about air toxics at airports across the county, and with 50 of the nation's busiest airports engaged in expansion programs, the process of discovery of what these toxics were and their effect on nearby populations, he believed should be analyzed. The director of the airports Aviation Division, at the time, Gina Marie Lindsey, who was also interviewed and asked about monitoring at Sea-Tac, managed to choke out her approval of such a discovery process. This news story would be the last time I would see Jim.

Although the ACC consultants found the carbon monoxide figures had been understated and the model manipulated to produce weird results, this issue would become part of the overall record just like my comments had been to date and nothing more. EPA's conditional approval of conformity, the Port's commitment to monitor the air, FAA's plan to phase out noisy jets and an overall pathetic lack of concern on water issues through the state permitting process seemed to satisfy all the requirements to progress to a Record of Decision (ROD) by FAA shortly after June of 1997. The process would now turn to the legal challenges, which, besides incorporating the air quality issues, had also gained standing on the process relating to the faulty alternative search by the PSRC, land use, wetland mitigation and water quality among others.

Foggy delays as the premise had caused enough concern by agencies for the ACC to spend money on a consultant to disprove it. The EIS had claimed that 44% bad weather delay would cost an incredible amount of money possibly billions in fuel as planes circled waiting to land in a constrained airport. The second leg of this fallacy purpose and need was that the same number of planes would come with or without the runway. But the expansion would have never been approved by EPA if it had been for capacity. The region would not have liked it as much or been able to sell it as well, or shove it down our throats as effectively as they did since it was for safe landings in bad weather. Jim was the only one who would have been able to get them to admit capacity and it didn't happen.

I suppose they could have used more light aircraft in any scenario they wanted to show less pollution and blinders would have gone on and agencies would have seen it as a win for lower emissions in the future. Maybe the consultants are hypnotists? I don't know…but they did a good job selling their obviously, plainly, ridiculous lie to everyone. In fact, even though we knew they were lying to us all along we were still calm and collected as we made our case for a semblance of a quality of life. We took it just like regular sheep.

Even though our group could at times stand back and laugh at the lunacy, we knew this folly was about to fall on us and we would have to pay the price so we were hopeful that through certification by the Governor, wetland permitting by Army Corps and the MOA for monitoring air Jim had secured before leaving, there might still be someone to champion our cause and reason would prevail.

I would now move into a phase of working with Ecology on the air quality monitoring and met Doug* who was to be in charge of this process. I was still working for RCAA, presently, paying bills, running the office, planning board meetings and filing. The filing alone could be a full-time job. There were, and still are, documents scattered all over the office. In the picture of the SEIS, the documents that stack nearly 3 feet high are stored in this office, along with scoping documents, planning documents, legal briefs, comprehensive plans, you name it, it is there…somewhere. The current administrative director, has done a great job in trying to organize and catalog the hundreds of documents, notes, letters, etc. I have asked him to find things for me during the writing of this book and he has been able, by some miracle of God, to find what I asked for. Truly amazing.

Chapter 10

CANCER

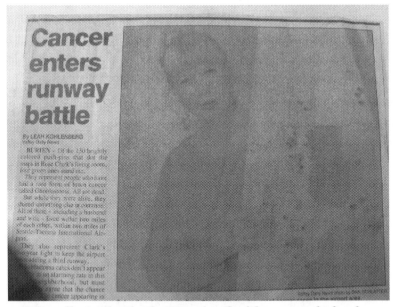

Cancer enters runway battle

By LEAH KOHLENBERG
Valley Daily News

BURIEN - Of the 130 brightly colored push-pins that dot the map in Rose Clark's living room, five greens ones stand out.

They represent people who have had a rare form of brain cancer called Glioblastoma. All are dead.

But while they were alive, they shared something else in common. All of them - including a husband and wife - lived within two miles of each other, within two miles of Seattle-Tacoma International Airport.

They also represent Clark's greatest fight to keep the airport from adding a third runway...

"The pollution levels of a 747 takeoff is like setting the local gas station on fire and then flying it overhead."[2]

Rose had put out questionnaires into the airport area asking people to volunteer information about their health. She learned that

[2] Quote from Claudio Parazzoli, CASE member and Boeing physicist

98

a large number of people had cancer. She put this information onto a map with colored push pins which indicated the type of cancer and deaths from cancer. Rose's cancer map interested me because I believed the huge emission load from jets at Sea-Tac were behind the problem. Audrey had worked at an elementary school which is located only about 10 blocks from the easternmost runway to the northeast of the airport. Most of the winds come from the southwest traveling off the Puget Sound to the northeast, which invariably carried most of the emissions during the year to this Riverton Heights neighborhood. Audrey had developed a brain tumor and was aware of several neighbors and co-workers at Riverton Heights Elementary school who had developed glioblastoma brain tumors and subsequently died from them.

During the EIS process I wrote lists of people for Rose from these survey forms. I was shocked by some of the information. Both adults, a husband and wife, had died of the glioblastoma brain tumor. Another family lost both the husband and wife, child and even the dog to cancer.

Dr. Olin of Sweden who, in 1986, had found incidences of brain tumors at a higher rate around sewage treatment plants, refineries and airports wrote:

"'Working at an airport' and 'living near a municipal sewage treatment plant' are two items that display an association with astrocytomas in the analysis. Organic compounds, particularly PCHs, (polycyclic hydrocarbons) are present everywhere but possibly in higher concentrations in such environments. PCH has long been known to be capable of inducing glial tumors, at least through direct local application, in animals [Swenberg, 1977].

In a study on brain tumors in children and the occupational exposure of parents, Peters and coworkers [Peters and Preston-Martin, 1981] found an excess of brain tumors in a supplementary registry study among men employed in such companies. To our knowledge, this is the only previously described association between aircraft/airports and astrocytomas."[37]

There is no safe level of PCH. The ASIL is extremely low at .00048 micrograms per cubic meter. The Ports analysis of soot containing pyrene which is a polycyclic aromatic hydrocarbon, (PAH) closely related to PCH at 2.5 mg/swab completely glossed over the significance of this finding and its potential for serious health effects. Nobody really knows what the swab is either. Is it a test tube or a cue-tip? It is unclear what the 2.5 has as a relationship to anything. Testing methods used on this soot are not disclosed. But it appears to me that analysis of spider web was probably visual observation rather than lab testing. Other soot was deemed 'too large' to be from jet engine combustion. It seems to me that this 'large soot' could have been many fine soot put together but most importantly, there was no written analysis of what was in the soot. Even though there are markers for many types of emissions used to identify a source, there are none for jet fuel. Many proprietary chemicals in Jet-A have never been disclosed. Therefore, the findings which rule out soot from jets cannot rule out soot from jets. At properties analyzed, there are no other industrial sources producing soot besides the jets unless soot is traveling ten miles from the nearest industrial area in Georgetown (which also has an airport and where PAH was found at higher rates than anywhere else in the region analyzed during a 2002 EPA grant study) against most prevailing winds and going uphill several hundred feet. If anything, it is most likely soot from jets than anything else.

The Riverton Heights neighborhood is outside of the corridor for buy-out homes the airport purchases for noise exposure, but it had been purchased and fenced off by the Port anyway. Audrey believes it was because of the brain tumors.

I had found another study of emissions, almost by accident, which was discussed in one of the planning documents Minnie had given me. In 1973 a resident living on the west side of the airport had a monitoring van belonging to King County sit in his driveway for a month. Environmental Systems Labs (ESL) out of California had sampled oxidants, along with particulates, carbon monoxide and sulfur. Air quality experts I asked thought the oxidants discussed in this report might be the precursors to ozone, nitrogen oxides and hydrocarbons.

ESL contained a number of recommendations based upon the high pollutant counts, all of which have been completely ignored. One was to avoid grinding industry which would add to the particulate problem. If particulate was high in 1973, is it possible eighty tons of dust from building the third runway, 57 double haulers on the road each hour combined with the annual 60 tons of jet particulate might be worse in 1995? Since hydrocarbon levels were also high, they recommended to not even build a gas station here. Ten more gas stations later, the odor is worse. ESL noted:

> "The only serious air quality problem is associated with the high hydrocarbon levels which are the major source of complaints regarding odors and are potential precursors to oxidant (ozone) formation."[38]

In 1995, Toni Turner, Noise Abatement Assistant responded to a resident's letter admitting:

> "A high number of jet aircraft operations may increase the smell of jet fuel odor and depending on weather conditions, localities around the Airport may notice the odor more."[39]

Again as far back as 1973 the recommendation from ESL:

> "In the interim, fuel additives, modified ground operations, and fuel vapor recovery systems are potential methods for reducing hydrocarbon emissions at SEA-TAC."[40]

Installing something as simple as vapor recovery, which has been recommended in independent reports for decades, is still not even being considered by the Port environmental staff. Senior environmental program supervisor, Russ Simonson recently responded to my request to install vapor recovery this way:

> "With the fuel hydrant system and closed tanks at the jet fuel tank farm, jet fuel exposure to the atmosphere at Sea-Tac is very limited. That said; the primary reason that a vapor recovery system has not been planned is for the fact that jet fuel has such a low vapor pressure that even when exposed to the atmosphere, the evaporative emissions are minute.
>
> We will continue to monitor any advancements that are made in available equipment and procedures to lessen any impact that our tenant's practices of fuel dispensing may have on the environment."[41]

These kerosene odors couldn't possibly be minute if people living two miles away can smell it. They are pumping nearly two million gallons of jet A fuel each day and even though they have admitted they know about the kerosene odors, they are completely unconcerned and uncommitted to mitigate although expressed in various recommendations for over three decades.

After reviewing the future expected increases in nitrogen oxide emissions the ESL authors made another interesting comment:

> "In section 5.5 we noted that even though hydrocarbon levels were very high, NOx levels were fairly low, and hence oxidant was not expected to be a significant problem. This conclusion may not carry over in the future because NOx levels are predicted to increase significantly."[42]

They were absolutely correct in their prediction regarding nitrogen oxide emissions. According to a 2003 report by Northeast States for Coordinated Air Use Management, in the time period 1970 to 1998, nitrogen oxide emissions from aircraft increased by 133% while all other industry including automobiles increased by 3% or less.[43]

"For example, while the number of registered automobiles in the U.S. has grown from 90 million to approximately 200 million from 1970 to 1998, NOx emissions have remained close to 1970 levels."[44]

We could then assume that oxidant or ozone levels would now also be a problem. With this increase in nitrogen oxide emissions from jet operations and 3% for cars, it makes no sense at all that the EIS concluded cars are the primary pollution source of concern at Sea-Tac Airport. It makes no sense to me that when PSCAA tells the public to drive less or not mow the lawn during an air pollution episode, a 747 still takes off producing emission levels equal to 4 million mowers, an amount nearly double the total housing units in the state.

ESL concluded:

"Around airports, land uses which are compatible with respect to noise may or may not be compatible with respect to air quality."[45]

Then in direct contradiction of the EIS:

"Airplanes are and will continue to be the major source of air pollution near SEA-TAC. Accordingly, it is natural to explore ways of reducing emissions by aircraft before other methods."[46]

The conclusions of this report, although now over 35 years old, are still very applicable today and have been reaffirmed by more current independent analysis. Yet not one recommendation has been implemented. Not one warning has been heeded. More jets, more cars, more gas stations, more particulate loading projects, more hydrocarbon producing parking garages, everything to be avoided has been added at a frenzied pace. Out of curiosity, I researched the property details of the home with the ESL monitoring van and found out the homeowner had listed and sold his home within one month after the study was released. Not a surprise. He was a legislator who later became a county councilmember. He had never mentioned this study to Liz who lived a few doors down and a friend of Minnie's group who had considered herself a good friend of this politician and his family. This politician, although conscious of a problem he quickly reacted to by moving his family away, never mentioned it to me either when I helped him campaign for re-election as a councilmember in 1984. Liz continued to live in the neighborhood and later developed leukemia. They both lived not too far from the family who had lost all members including the dog to cancer.

I called King County and asked why homes hadn't been bought out, why had people been left to become certain victims of these emission problems. They referred me once again to the Port. Their draft conformity responses to comments admitted:

> "As would be expected, the acreage containing Sea-Tac Airport emits a greater level of air pollution than the average acre within King County for specific pollutants."[47]

Midway Airport's toxics analysis concluded that jets were 99% responsible for the predicted cancer risk increase in the communities near the airport. Nobody disputed this technical, credible EPA risk analysis. On the other hand, in answer to PSCAA's request for a risk assessment Sea-Tac's EIS claimed that cars are the primary polluter of concern with aircraft contributing only 10% and further stated that;

"***cancer risk*** estimates are not meant to be representative of actual risk. Instead, they are meant to be used in a relative sense, to compare risks among pollutants."[48]

Personally, I think people are more interested in knowing if they are hanging in the air outside their front door and going to kill them!

MFG had found cancer causing emissions in the neighborhoods around Sea-Tac at levels much higher than the acceptable limits according to state law. Midway's report had said cancer cases would be higher around the airport. Ecology's report indicated surprise at the high rate of emissions. In my mind important issues had been settled. Are there emissions and at rates expected to cause disease? Yes, reports had admitted the emissions were present in modeling (EPA's Midway, Ecology). Are they present in the neighborhoods? Yes, and at the rates expected to cause disease when air monitoring found them in the neighborhoods (MFG). Are there higher disease and death rates associated with these emissions? The dozens of push pins crammed into small areas on Rose's map made it look that way. So why wasn't anyone besides me talking about this problem? Why wasn't the media talking about it? Why didn't these agencies who are supposed to protect the public not doing something? EPA told me the report was too old to use. It expressed emissions in terms which were not even used anymore. PSCAA said the current EIS was the most accurate study to date and it indicated there was not really a problem. Midway's study documented concern about a compound that was not even monitored in 1973, nor was it included in the current EIS. I was then, and still occasionally doubt my own conclusions mostly because nobody is reacting the way I think people should react when people might be harmed.

Chapter 11

ECOLOGY

Jim had secured funding and a commitment in a Memorandum of Agreement (MOA) signed by EPA Department of Ecology (Ecology), PSCAA and the Port for an air quality analysis. The three agencies would lend aspects of their individual expertise to the study with funding from the Port. The project design would be headed by Ecology's Doug*, possibly one of the most skilled air quality engineers in the region. Working for the state, he has been involved in many major pollution discovery programs for the past decade or longer and is always willing to share endless details of these processes. As the primary engineer on the discovery team, he wanted to hold a meeting with interested parties from EPA, PSCAA and citizens. I arranged for this group to meet at the RCAA office.

Two representatives from PSCAA showed up. Although in charge of compiling regional air pollution monitoring data and probably very technically skilled with the ability to lend valuable resources to the current MOA, they were the ones who had conducted the residue lab tests for the resident in the flight path who claimed the oily soot was eating the paint off his boat but had found nothing more than natural material and fungus. They were also the most unhelpful agency of all when I had previously went to them with my concerns about emissions even though two of their staff had

106

inadvertently provided me with most of the technical information on air pollution facts I now possessed. They argued with the validity of comparing the short term hydrocarbon monitoring with an annual ASIL although reason and logic dictated it would be that high all year long. They wanted to fall on the side of wishful thinking, best case and trust the Port's consultant's work. They wouldn't stand by their previous State Implementation Plan predictions of emissions for Sea-Tac which were almost triple the EIS figures for jets. I had previously thought Ecology was the most unhelpful because they didn't even take the time to formally comment on the runway EIS, possibly the biggest project this decade.

However, Ecology's Doug impressed me as a truly concerned person, someone who really cared about his job and about the health of people. With several degrees in various fields related to emissions and testing, he likes to talk about the process and gives wonderful detailed technical facts. I would sometimes get lost trying to listen to him but was afraid to interrupt. He takes very few breaks when he starts talking and much of what he says is probably way over the head of most people, so would tend to bore anyone not completely interested in this subject or him. After our first meeting, many of the group including PSCAA, EPA, my boss and Bob representing the Port basically said their well wishes for an interesting program and did not come to any more meetings or our field trips, which was fine with me.

Doug and I, along with another technician from his department went out driving one day to look for sites for the permanent air monitoring stations. There would be two trailers placed at each end of the airport. One would house a particulate monitor, nitrogen dioxide (NO2), wind speed and temperature equipment. The other, would measure particulate once in six days and include a nephelometer along with NO2. A nephelometer measures light scatter as a way of detecting dust particles in the air. If I had known more about the nephelometer I would have insisted it be placed in a different spot than where it ended up. Placement on each end of the airport, to capture upwind/downwind conditions is pretty standard. My idea for the best spots would be slightly to the southwest on the south end and slightly to the northeast on the north end because most of the wind models I had previously seen had winds predominately from the southwest. Winds blowing past the south monitor would theoretically show low readings, while the north monitor would then capture the higher readings for comparison of what the airport was adding to the air shed, or so I thought.

Doug wanted to place badge samplers along the fence of the airport property to try to find the highest spot for NO. I asked why monitor at the fence since the Port had earlier claimed this was not an area of public exposure so didn't matter in relationship to the federal standards. He told me that even if a worm living at the fence line might be harmed by these emissions, the law would apply. His team was engaged in placing carbon monoxide monitors along the nearby street where modeling had indicated violations. They were also trying to get them placed along the curb at the airport drives but meeting resistance from the Port during this busy period.

While the air monitoring project was getting underway, Ecology issued a certification of air and water quality standards on behalf of Governor Lowry, who at the time was apparently unwilling to do so for whatever reason. Certification is a federal requirement where the governor guarantees in writing that the project design and construction will not violate any known air and water quality standards. Legislators and the representative to congress from the airport district area complained to the United States Secretary of Transportation that this was not what was required in the federal rule. An agency can only certify on behalf of the governor if that governor is incapacitated. Strangely, the requisite certification was three pages of conditions. An agreed order was entered into between the Port and Ecology requiring monitoring and modeling of the ground contaminated 'on airport' sites to predict future fate and transport. The team of water quality experts at Ecology who had investigated the leaking hydrant lines, jet fuel on the aquifer, etc., during scoping for the EIS had genuine concerns about those conditions. The agreed order, the air quality memorandum of agreement, feasibility of an underground aquifer under the new runway plateau, water issues, further noise mitigation measures, were some of the conditional requirements written into this certification. Not only had the wrong people written it, it failed to certify anything as is required. In fact, Ecology, who presently certified the project's compliance, were the ones who previously found violations of both air and water quality standards in the past.

The air monitoring program had just begun, the agreed order hadn't started, additional noise measures recommended by the Noise Panel and required by PSRC's rewritten resolution were still on the drawing table. Wetland destruction hadn't been permitted, haul routes hadn't been chosen, but by gum, someone was going to shove this thing through. Our CASE group also wrote letters to all our US representatives pointing out the guidelines of the federal certification rule had been ignored. Then we had an election and a new governor, Gary Locke, took office. Apparently, our citizen pressure and that of our representatives was successful in transferring the responsibility for certification to the proper Chief Executive of the State as the federal rule requires.

Governor Locke had been one of the county executives who had voted to change the resolution and approve the third runway as a member of the PSRC. Now as governor, he would certify the project with the quirky conditional approval written verbatim as had been drafted by Ecology. The certification however, is the usual federal next step after a ROD is issued which frees up the federal agencies to begin pouring money into the project. So the project would start even though air and water quality laws could by no means be guaranteed for compliance with federal law.

The process of demolition of homes and clearing the way for the millions of tons of dirt would not overlap with the air quality analysis as I had hoped. All the dust from hauling and dumping would not make it to the particulate samplers. But we still had many avenues of hope left for common sense to prevail. The attorneys had filed their briefs shortly after the ROD was issued. The Army Corps had already written adversarial comments on the wetland destruction. It didn't look good for borrow pits on site from the State Department of Mining. Minnie's group was stirring up trouble with the State Auditor on the financial problems with the Port's business practices. Minnie was finding out the Port had violated requirements of their noise mitigation grant process. Rose and Audrey were getting air time on TV news with the cancer map and as a result, the State Department of Public Health was getting ready to be involved with discovery of illnesses in the community.

Meanwhile, working at the Regional Commission on Airport Affairs (RCAA) was becoming my tool for outreach. I had not intended to use the business for connecting to other groups from around the world, it just started to creep in on me from the RCAA web site and e-mail outreach. Nearly every day there was some message through the e-mail or on the phone line from some other group wanting to find out what and how our group was doing. Many of the messages proclaimed that we were the most sophisticated group around because we had the web site. Our ACC cities also had a large amount of financial resources dedicated to the legal costs of challenging the runway. People were watching and waiting to hear good news from us since we were so well organized, or so they thought, and I was more than curious to find out what was going on with these other groups.

I couldn't understand why nobody at RCAA had ever discussed these other groups with our CASE group before. To me it seemed like a great extra tool to network with these groups and find out what had been their successes, if any. I would also be able to share the air quality information with them when, as I was sure would happen, the air monitoring found violations of the federal standards. If it were happening here, it would surely be happening everywhere else.

Doug had gone door to door in the neighborhood to the northeast trying to find a home for the permanent monitor but people wanted money to house it and the budget was too tight. He told me that everyone he talked to was sick which concerned him. He had intended to put an air toxics monitor out there on his own time to try and find out what was in the air. He was told by his department manager that if he found something nobody could do anything about it so don't bother.

The south trailer would sit in a depression at Tyee Golf Course within a few hundred yards of the runway end, where most takeoffs occur. This would be the home of the nephelometer along with a particulate monitor which would capture particles one day out of six. Doug who seemed so willing to find the truth never discussed the nephelometer monitor with me. Because I completely trusted his judgment, I never asked.

Riverton Heights neighborhood which had been bought out by the Port, became the northeast site for the other trailer. There was power and a fence to protect the equipment from vandalism and theft. Although somewhat removed from the airport, exposure was thought to be good since it was at nearly the same elevation and downwind. Below this area a lightly traveled state highway ran to the east. The spot where heavy airport traffic merged onto this highway was over a hill about a half mile away from the monitor and would not be considered to interfere with capturing mostly jet emissions.

Historically, Beacon Hill had been the home of the areas only permanent Nitrogen Dioxide (NO2) monitoring station. This site has historically been designated the highest in the region for NO2 measuring anywhere from .017 annually to .020 with the annual federal standard at .053. PSCAA had once told me there were probably no violations of the federal standard for NO2 occurring anywhere. In fact, they would be surprised if any monitor had more than half the standard, above .027. It is probably monitored more for its contribution to violations of the federal ozone standard rather than for its immediate effects as a poisonous gas.

In 1994 a monitoring van used by the University of Washington performed an NO2 saturation study of the county traveling from the northern part of Seattle, through town, and then down through Beacon Hill, Renton, Kent and Auburn toward the permanent ozone monitor in Enumclaw. The Enumclaw ozone monitor had recorded violations of the federal ozone standard over the course of the last several years. The study was meant to determine if there were other areas more suitable than Beacon Hill for a permanent monitor. With the push for regional attainment of the standards, it was important at this time in history for the team to look for other highs, and maybe even a source. The rates detected by the van were relatively low and steady, high at Beacon Hill, which has no sources of its own except is over flown by aircraft from three airports. Rates decreased along the plateau that travels to the east of the airports in Renton and Kent, rising again as the van descended the hill toward Enumclaw. The areas near Boeing Field and Sea-Tac were completely bypassed by the monitoring van. I had argued it was purposeful, Ecology countered it was an accidental omission. Strange since just three years earlier, their own report of Sea-Tac emissions suggested they should use the van around the airport to get a better idea of what is out there.

The SEIS response to comments had admitted Sea-Tac Airport contributed more ozone precursors by acre than any other acre in the county. I had no trouble understanding why those badge samplers were coming up with high readings and I am not surprised that the ozone monitor in Enumclaw is picking up violations of the standard. It is directly in the path of a trough, a valley where all emissions from two airports with over 600,000 annual operations between them will end up if the wind is from the northwest, typical of warm summer weather which tends to turn NO and hydrocarbons into ozone. Jet engines produce massive amounts of NO. It's in all the literature, even admitted four times in the Port's own EIS. With 600 takeoffs per day, 400 of those being jets, the daily volume of NO might be nearly 10 tons at Sea-Tac alone, not spread out all over the county like cars but concentrated from a single source. If you have a huge polluter next to the monitor, it doesn't take a rocket scientist to figure out the relationship. These are big engines burning thousands of pounds of fuel just to take off. Ecology, on the other hand, didn't see it. They were scrambling around to figure out what was going on. In retrospect, if I had been more involved maybe things might have turned out differently. But for the time being, I was hopeful the study would take care of itself, violations would appear and the whole thing would be done. I was wrong.

Chapter 12

STATE AUDITOR

At some point in between processes of gain an inch, lose a mile, Minnie's C-6 issue which is the noise mitigation grant assurance requiring city approval of insulation programs became a topic the State Auditor agreed to look into. He was also willing to look at a number of other programs that had financial implications.

I had written to the State Department of Appraisal Licensing about what I perceived to be weird and unusual practices in the appraisal and sale process of homes in the Transaction Assistance program. I had also complained to the Department of Real Estate Licensing about a conflict of interest with the Port's contract real estate agent.

The real estate agent had an active real estate office at the same time he was on contract to do work for the Port. Some in our group believed his contract with the Port didn't allow him to be involved with both. His knowledge about home prices in the Transaction Assistance program would give him an inside track for private profiteering. For example, when the homes in the Transaction Assistance program failed to sell during the first four months or so of private marketing of the home, the Port would then purchase the home from the homeowner at the agreed price set by the contract appraiser and then the home would be marketed for however long it took to sell with the agent incrementally dropping the price every two months and receiving the assigned real estate fee at the end. What is to stop him from purposely discouraging a possible private sale, forcing the home into the last period bringing the home price down, making it a much better deal for him and prospective clients? Wouldn't someone naturally want to wait?

Before I had signed up for Transaction Assistance, I thought I would first do some research on the program. I asked a real estate friend of the CASE group if she could pull up sales data for some of the homes located in Thunderbird Estates which I knew were eligible for Transaction Assistance.

Thunderbird Estates is a residential neighborhood which sits high on a hill in Des Moines. The roads wind around neighborhoods with cul-de-sacs everywhere, discouraging through traffic. Many of the homes are brick with over 2,000 square feet. All the homes I researched had 90 to 180 degree views of the Puget Sound and Olympic Mountains. But these are all near 20th Avenue South, one and a half mile directly from the runway end. Most takeoffs go right over these homes in south flow which occurs about 60 to 70% of the year. Average noise levels are 75 DNL and above, considered unhealthful by EPA standards. Many of these homes were built in the 1960's when few jets flew over long before the airport expanded to two runways adding 100,000 operations

One of the fact sheets from this neighborhood caught my attention immediately. It was a home assessed for $250,000 which had sold for $165,000. Granted, assessments can be off, but in this up-market period in 1995, with homes quickly appreciating in value, it didn't make sense that there was nearly 100,000 dollars difference. I contacted the homeowner and asked them if they would be willing to share information with me on what happened. They had been told by the Port that their appraisal was private and could not be shared with anyone other than the assigned agents. I told them that I was a leader of a community group affected by aircraft noise and was interested in the program details with the hope of getting regulators involved to scrutinize the Port's practices and misdeeds if any. They wrote out a note giving me permission and mailed it to me.

The contract appraiser had used the wrong value for square feet. They used basement value for upstairs living space and unfinished value for finished basement square feet. They underestimated the basement square feet. They gave no value whatsoever for the view, they missed a fireplace, gave no credit for upgrades, no value for the level yard they called a slope and made several other mistakes. In re-calculating the value, at least $30,000 dollars had been missed. The Port's appraisal was $220,000. The homeowner had paid for an independent appraisal which came in at $250,000. Their appraiser and the Port negotiated a compromise at $232,000. This home, selling anywhere else besides the flight path, would have been worth at least 100 thousand more. The comparables used were noise affected with few comparative features besides size.

The Port kept $23,200 for real estate fees. If the house sold for $165,000 the Port should receive 16,500 or 10%, the amount they require for the listing and selling agents, where does the extra money go? During the first marketing period, an offer of $220,000 was made and the Port refused to accept it. They never negotiated on the set price, even though the $220,000 was the original price they had set in the first place. Accepting this offer would have been a far better proposition for everyone, the market, sales prices and stability for value. By not accepting this offer, the home was forced into the last phase of marketing, where the Port's contract agent makes money, the buyer gets a much better deal and home prices are further deflated. I provided examples to the Department of Real Estate Licensing on this and several other homes that were sold for almost $100,000 less than the value assigned by the appraiser.

Another home in the Transaction Assistance program had never sold during the standard marketing period so the Port kept it. Where does the real estate fee go then? How about that 80% federal and 20% local which pays for the program through FAR (Federal Aviation Regulation) Part 150[3] grant funds, the ones Minnie wanted investigated. When the Port buys a home for $232,000 for instance, do they use 80% federal and when they sell it privately to some poor sucker, do they keep the whole $165,000 or give back a portion to the federal funds in the resale? The Port has said the money goes back into the program but my question is where in the program? How about reimbursing some of the real estate fees not used in the final sale back to the original homeowner? Practices I viewed as illegal, unethical, at least questionable, the Department of Real Estate licensing felt were just fine.

The Department of Appraisal Licensing gave more regard to my concerns about the contract appraiser and the errors I found. They contacted me and said they would investigate which would take about a month. After a month I contacted them and asked how it was going. They said they had a hard time finding the appraiser. They had quit the business, closed shop and moved to Florida. They were awaiting their response although it had passed the deadline.

Eventually, the State did send a response to me, which included a letter from the appraiser saying they had followed the terms of their contract with the Port, and the state agreed they had obeyed the terms which somehow absolved them of responsibility for errors in judgment, using devalued homes for comparables and numerous mistakes in calculations. Maybe I should have made my original complaint to the Department of Contract Terms if there were such a thing. It isn't bad enough that the homes were devalued by the airport operations, they were further devalued by the practices of the appraiser and real estate agent. Since these processes are not overseen by anyone, but run by the Port, for the Port and only for

---

[3] FAA funding regulation for implementation of noise mitigation programs

the Port, with an internal appeal process also run by the Port, is it any wonder they are getting away with such unusual practices? The downward trend in property values would continue because all these homes are used as comparables outside the Port's programs. Homes across the street from the noise zone, which many believe are just as noisy as homes in the zone, are used as comparables for values within the zone.

Since I believed the state departments of real estate and appraisal licensing had ignored genuine questionable practices with large financial implications in their evaluation of these two contractors, I thought it would be a good idea for the State Auditor to look it over and Minnie invited me along.

It was Minnie who had been granted the meeting and it was Minnie who was so well prepared. She had thoroughly investigated the home insulation program and found inequities. Not only had the Port violated their grant agreement, they were using the money in a very irresponsible manner. She found that they had insulated a home worth $100,000 dollars at the edge of the insulation program, barely above 65 DNL, with $40,000 dollars worth of materials and labor, while more valuable homes, more affected by noise received $3,000 dollars worth. In one case, they refused to replace view windows that were too large, while insulating a shack not even in the noise zone. One woman had her house only half insulated on one side which faced the flight path. Others were experiencing problems like windows pulling away from the wall, broken seals, mold problems developing from the home being too tightly sealed with minimal air circulation. These problems the Port was in no way obligated to pay to fix because homeowners had waived their rights to recourse for problems stemming from the insulation.

Minnie's number one complaint; the grant approval was based upon the cities' written agreement and approval allowing the Port to do the work, an agreement that had not been executed in any of the cities where work had been performed. This should have nullified the grant, should have got the Port into big trouble and should have opened the door for homeowners to have their problems fixed, the agreements voided and their easement revoked.

Instead, when the cities were told they had this right, they summarily waived it. The FAA later claimed, after our district congressman Adam Smith brought it up on a Federal level, that they had a verbal agreement with the Port to bypass that part of the grant agreement. I would have thought it was a pretty big deal that a special purpose district didn't have permission to do work in a city when that condition was a requirement to receive federal funding for that work. Apparently, these days when government doesn't seem to want to represent anybody but just wants to manage your money, it's no big deal. The possibility that homeowners' waivers might have been made void allowing them to have shoddy work re-done or be compensated for noise damages the expert panel found to still be occurring, didn't take precedence over cities potentially becoming laden with the task of taking care of their residents. When the cities decided not to get involved, that was it for Minnie. She quit the fight altogether after this.

The State Auditor's office eventually absolved the Port from any wrong doing with all of the problems we brought to their attention. So everything continues as it always was, people are harmed, agencies get rich, nothing gets fixed and the polluter pays rule still only applies to all other industry.

Today, homeowners are complaining at meetings that the windows are fogged, pulling away from the walls, they have mold and mildew but are told they have no recourse for repairs or replacements because of the waivers. Many of the companies that built the windows and affixed insulation are no longer in business. Worse than this, homeowners might have been told they can bring this up at the FAR 150 meetings. You know what that means? They will have to wait two years to find out the answer. Meanwhile they have to live in their subnormal situation. The Port and FAA are currently talking about adding air conditioners, something that should have been done years ago, especially in the schools. This would help with the air pollution problems they never acknowledge but know about. Air conditioners can pull particulates out of the air as well as keep moisture from building up. Air conditioners have been installed into the windows at the Maywood School where the Port's noise remedy office is now located. This school located south of the airport was closed due to high noise levels. Funny how the Port's staff working there somehow warrants consideration, but the thousands of school children in other nearby schools don't.

These types of things, like vapor recovery and hush houses have been being talked about for decades and no movement forward has ever occurred. A lot of these types of things remind me of the reliever airport discussions which seem to be another tactic to wear people out. We get hopeful for a moment, relax and then find out two years later they didn't approve any of it. We have to find a new tact to get help and we're back on the road to nowhere once again.

Maybe in two years we will find out they decided not to include air conditioners and then what do we do? Complain to our congressman, wait two years for a letter writing barrage which finds nobody is in charge so no help is available. Then what? How many times can people run in circles chasing after wind?

Chapter 13

HOK

Some of the costs and losses which would be experienced as a result of the third runway at Sea-Tac were tallied up by a consultant, Hellmuth, Obata and Kassebaum, (HOK) contracted by the State of Washington. Their final estimate of losses to the local cities and communities was 2.95 billion dollars. Much of this included buying out homes and redevelopment of land in the flight paths to the north and south of the third runway. Thirteen years later, this has not begun. The EIS had estimated approximately 50 million in losses considering many of the same issues discussed by HOK, a vast underestimation.

The FAA and Port claimed that the delays resulting from fog in the future, with increased operations, would at one time amount to an annual 176 million in fuel costs by 2010 with 425,000 operations, and two runways. Planes would be idling and circling the skies waiting for clearance to land or a gate to use. In 2006 and still no third runway, average delay with 445,000 operations was a mere .50% weather related attributable to Sea-Tac. 7% delay was attributed to other airports.

In fact, delay had gone down with more operations since 1996 when it was 384,000 with 1% delay according to the consultants the

ACC hired compared to .5 with 445,000 in 2006. Nothing near the 44% the EIS stated. The 7% is more typical of total system delays that occur at other airports which have nothing to do with fog at Sea-Tac. This makes the purpose and need of the airport expansion and over a billion dollars spent, mostly on dirt to date, based upon a completely false premise. So, they had been wrong, or were they misleading on purpose?

I personally think lying to people is immoral and unethical.

Thousands of community members, consultants, experts and cities questioned the bad weather delay assumptions used in the EIS. The Port and FAA were evasive at best constantly insisting the costs of delay were enormous. At the rate they were going, they might have been able to realize 525,000 annual operations with less than 7% delay which was the 2030 lifetime expected maximum with a third runway, or so they claimed. If you calculate an annual operations figure from the 43.9 doubled for each mode the consultant claimed was average day/level use (although using the 43.9 as a total was the operational figure they had in 1995, approximately 384,710, an argument I used with Jim to convince him they were lying) it's possible for 770,000 annual operations with two runways. So it couldn't really be for forecasts unless there were constraints on certain times of day. With no night-time curfew for flights at Sea-Tac like they have at Dulles in DC, that doesn't make sense. It couldn't be for a fog problem because that didn't exist. The only thing that made sense to me was for peak hour push.

In retrospect, the airport lost nothing in fuel costs during the eleven years prior to the third runway. From the ROD to 2008, none of the airports predictions of constraint, bad weather, airport crowding and congestion were validated while during the same time period the communities lost property values, road stability, hundreds of residents, tax base and businesses, while costs of services, rebuilding, restructuring and upgrading schools cost cities and citizens millions.

HOK did not add in health care costs associated with the noise and emissions from the airport. Contemporary studies did estimate there would be increased health care costs and time lost from work due to exposure to air pollution but extrapolating data from fluctuating sources then applying it somehow to Sea-Tac was not within the scope of this analysis. HOK wrote:

"Given the amount of information available and the project's budget and time constraints, it was not possible to calculate the mitigation costs for potential impacts associated with the remaining environmental measures (wetlands, floodplains, aquifer, air quality, etc.) Additional studies should be commissioned to determine the potential impacts associated with the airport's proposed project. [49]

They also did not add in the costs to insulate 26 schools. Relocation of Occupational Skills Center (OSC) and Highline High School were not mentioned in the study, but would be nearly next door to the expanded airport. In one spot, the EIS had mentioned OSC should be moved but nobody has talked about it for years even though it is right next to the fence-line of the airport. Four schools were mentioned as needing relocation/replacement although the cost of doing so was not included in the analysis. Years later the district did receive funds from the airport to insulate and rebuild some of the schools. However, a new tax levy would fund the majority of these costs where the communities most affected, and depreciated by losses of tax base, would pay the bill. HOK did mention that redevelopment of removed uses would be the responsibility of the mitigated costs carried by the local jurisdictions.

"Mitigation of these neighborhoods are estimated to be approximately $1.9 billion – 80% of the total environmental impacts. These 5 neighborhoods are the closest to the proposed project and will experience significant impacts, due primarily to noise and vibration of aircraft operations.

The $1.9 billion figure represents the cost to relocate neighborhood residents and redevelop the area."[50]

We thought the region should pay for it all. In fact, the region should get their own airport. Our county has two. The three other counties have none, an unfair burden considering the majority of the users (96% according to HOK) come from outside the areas affected by Sea-Tac operations.

There didn't seem to be anyone on board to require the people living in the new flight paths be bought out and removed or at least insulated before the new runway was built. This is a mitigation that has never begun, simply because the third runway was to be a limited use, bad weather runway and wouldn't be used very often according to the Port's EIS. But what if the runway were used all the time? Would those people who awoke one day to find themselves in a war zone as I had years earlier be told it was their fault for moving or staying there?

Even though HOK did a very thorough job of tallying up losses, these became nothing more than talking points for the cities to request mitigation funds from various interests who would benefit most from the runway. Nothing has been done for the residents even though the PSRC had promised to pursue legislation which would financially compensate the victims of their decision to approve the runway.

The victims are still waiting.

Chapter 14

Army Corps of Engineers

Again, we had another opportunity to spend the better part of our lives to put together well thought out and well written documentation on why the government shouldn't approve stupid, costly, extravagant, unjustifiable, limited use public works projects meant to destroy so much while giving so little in return. The Army Corps of Engineers were now accepting public comments on the permit process for the wetland destruction. The Port had got a bargain on some land in Auburn and wanted to move the wetlands they were going to destroy at Sea-Tac many miles away. They cited bird attractants so in-basin mitigation of wetland destruction would be dangerous.

FAA's rule for bird attractants says water bodies should not be located within 10,000 feet of an active runway. If that rule applied here, the Puget Sound would be too close, so would the pond the Port built to hold water at the end of the second runway. All streams, and four lakes were all too close. That didn't stop them from building the first or second runway. I think this bird attractant language is another excuse for the FAA to justify paving over more lakes and rivers near airports with the hope of allowing airport sponsors to turn them into money making cargo warehousing or parking lots. Except for the stream or creek they need for their open chemical sewer to drain glycol, oil, solvents and other wastes off airport property. Granted, bird strikes are a real concern for approaching and departing aircraft, this is true. But if the FAA was truly concerned about this, they would have closed runway 22 Right at John F. Kennedy International (JFK) in New York years ago. This runway deposits departing planes directly over a wildlife preserve/bird sanctuary where in 1975 a DC-10 aborted takeoff after a bird strike, went off the runway and caught fire. Fortunately all passengers exited the plane safely but the aircraft was completely destroyed. JFK leads the nation in bird strikes with 1811 reported from 1990 to 2008.

This is something that doesn't make sense to me...the rule only seems to apply after the fact, for expansion and development. It doesn't seem to carry any weight for existing facilities. Airports and the FAA are promoting an expansionist agenda, spending triple the cost on building runways at constrained existing facilities next to every major water body in the country, when good, cheap vacant desert land is readily available. I don't suppose the argument that it's too remote will work to deter building in the middle of nowhere. It's a plane...it can go to remote locations. Take a little commuter plane or a train to complete your trip. It takes more time yes, but according to FAA's own guidance on bird attractants, it would be safer. That way our little city doesn't have to host all of you. Were shriveling up from plane exhaust, and running low on gum, give us a break.

Army Corps didn't completely accept the bird attractant rule as reasonable justification for forever removing waters of the United States.

I wrote what I thought were wonderful comments to the Army Corps and met with one of their experts, Muffy who was working on the project. For some silly reason, I though a regulator with the name "Muffy" would be friendly, which I think translates into kindhearted, concerned and caring, the kind of individual I really needed right now. But in my brief meeting with her, she seemed strictly military material, matter of fact and not willing to mess around with what would be my several week long dissertation on emission mischief. I could tell right away that my conformity fiasco was not the Corps' concern whatsoever. She did get back to me after talking to the FAA and let me know that, in her opinion, FAA and all parties involved had adequately addressed the conformity issue to the satisfaction of the EPA.

Yes, EPA approved conformity but only if you accept dozens of conditions, lies, manipulations of data, alteration of the fleet mix, mythical times in mode, a preposterously too low number of aircraft movements in comparison to the FAA's own forecasts, a lack of comparison to a realistic capacity increase, nobody caring and nobody in charge, then yes, EPA did approve conformity.

Here was the problem I was now facing. Of course it must be needed, the PSRC approved it. It must be environmentally friendly, EPA accepted it. It must be legal, the Governor certified it. The newspapers hadn't mentioned anything wrong with it. Representatives weren't passing any laws against it. It must be good. Muffy didn't want to hear why these professional, well educated experts had all been wrong. I can't blame her. If I were in her position I don't know how much time I would give someone like myself. I'm pretty sure I was starting to sound like a kook. Nobody else was talking about the problems I was bringing up. If what I were saying were true, wouldn't more people be involved? If I were so right on, why had the process gone this far? With a chance the air monitoring would find violations and the whole game might be off, I let it go. Putting the kind of effort necessary to make a tiny dent in the process had worn me out. At this time also, there were many experts working on the wetlands and water quality who knew far more than I did. My conformity issue might have been a distraction to the Corps. After all we still had the legal team involved in several challenges of the process and laws to hope and root for.

The Corps did require the Port to re-write their proposal with a plan for more in-basin mitigation, a better creek relocation plan, and a different water resource to supplement low-flows in the streams during summer rather than stealing it from the local water district. I took this opportunity to send in another stack of comments which included my first set which had been lost. This process took another year out of my life and the total now was nearly eight years in the 'cause.' I am also very thankful our collective groups, cities, RCAA and CASE along with Greg and local representatives had the talent and knowledge behind their water and wetland concerns to deter the use of contaminated dirt and out of basin mitigation. They helped craft a better creek relocation plan and overall protection of this vast aquatic resource area which includes drinking water aquifers and endangered salmon runs. I am sorry my issue had been rubber stamped as dead by EPA, but my brief day in the sun had passed and I needed to move on. Even if I had been a rocket scientist, it wouldn't have mattered. Credentialed experts in every field had already been ignored as much as me.

Property owners on the west side of the airport who were part of the buy-out group whose homes would soon be destroyed to make way for the many millions of metric tons of dirt were holding off on accepting what they felt were low offers from the Port on their homes and properties. One group at Lora Lake wanted to wait it out to force the Port to go into an eminent domain process. It was potentially a losing gamble for entrenched homeowners who might receive a better figure if they caused a delay in the process or receive less compensation if the Port moved quickly on eminent domain.

As properties were purchased and destroyed, more wetlands were discovered. During flight plan prior to the EIS, the region said Paine Field would lose 26 acres if considered for expansion instead of Sea-Tac which would lose zero. If all projects had ever been tallied together, adding the north area EPA disallowed early on, it would be over 40 acres of wetland impact and destruction for Sea-Tac's third runway. At a 2 to 1 replacement ratio, 80 acres would have had to be enhanced or created, equal to almost 1/3 the size of the existing airport. For in-basin, realistically, they would need to purchase another large chunk of inhabited city of Burien homes just to mitigate. But the airport doesn't usually add all projects together. They will wait and piecemeal the rest later so that the impacts look smaller. Nobody is going to go back and look at the EIS to see how they violated the National Environmental Policy Act on piecemeal projects. Nobody ever did understand they never added cumulative impacts properly. The EIS is a closed book according to any regulator who might be willing to look into it. Unfortunately, there has been no one since Jim who has been as willing to do so.

At this time in history, my life was starting to get out of control. I was way over my head in work, being a single mom, volunteering at the new school my children were attending, running CASE, keeping track of what I was supposed to do next. I was starting to have a troubling situation at the RCAA and it wasn't the mountains of papers wanting to swallow me alive either. I tell my children, there is always a brighter tomorrow. Be patient, you just have to wait for it. For now, it seemed all I could see were dark clouds. I had failed my group, my marriage, my resources were running low, and even though I was surrounded by people all day, I was suffering from loneliness.

Chapter 15

RCAA

The Regional Commission on Airport Affairs (RCAA) is an umbrella organization that considers itself the head of all the community groups fighting airport expansion. There are groups in Rainier Valley, one on Beacon Hill, another in Seattle and of course their mainstay, CASE.

RCAA received funding from the local cities through the Airport Communities Coalition (ACC). The funding came from a utility tax collection used to build the legal war-chest to fight airport expansion. At one time Federal Way to the south, was a member but I don't know what, if anything, was their individual financial contribution to the ACC or RCAA. Other contributing cities of Burien, Normandy Park and Des Moines made up the bulk of the ACC budget. The ACC also included the Highline School District, which was, at one time one of the largest and oldest school districts in the state.

From time to time during the course of the fight, letters would sometimes appear in the local small newspaper from community members who were concerned about the tax and how it was being spent. Most of these letters probably came from people who had an interest of some sort in seeing the expansion go through. While a resident of Federal Way, I was asked by a councilmember to make a presentation on why this collection was important. Anyone who lived in the area was already aware of the terrible losses and degradation going on in the neighborhoods as a direct consequence of effects of the existing airport. Expansion would make it worse and most locals knew this and were willing to fund a fight. But since RCAA received the controversial public money through the cities, their functions were strictly limited and spelled out by the ACC. ACC membership consisted of council members who changed over several times during the third runway battle. Many of the newer members didn't understand much of the history or future course of the litigation and on-going challenges. Each contract period brought about new in-fighting about whether RCAA should continue to receive funding, what it would be used for and what support, if any, RCAA could give to other community groups like CASE. Although it was important to me for ACC to continue to be funded, as their contribution to RCAA paid my salary, I was more concerned the attorneys would continue to be paid to stop the madness. I wasn't sure what benefit, if any, RCAA provided that could not be reproduced by CASE although sidetracking funding from cities for a grassroots organization was probably not going to happen.

RCAA consists of a board of directors, a paid writer for the newsletter, administrator for the web site an office staff person (me), and at one time, a well paid director who, under undisclosed, mysterious circumstances, resigned before the first EIS process was complete. He was given one years' pay at his departure so many citizens speculated he was forced out but nobody I have talked to knows for sure why he left.

It is my opinion that the RCAA might have been set up as a stop-gap between the citizens and the cities to take the thousands of calls and complaints from citizens freeing up the cities to do city business. As a former call taker, I believe this is a bad idea along with the airport taking their own noise complaint calls. Nobody in a position of authority who can or is willing to do anything about all these calls is aware of the tremendous load of heartache and suffering going on in the communities.

At one point in my tenure as office administrator, a new director of the board changed my title to interim office administrator. I asked whether my job were now temporary and did not receive a response. My relationship with the new director was particularly strained. I think it had something to do with my leading the citizen group and taking charge of many situations that came up in the office, which made the former director happy but now maybe made the new director feel I was usurping his authority. He arrived one day and found me having a phone conversation that was just ending. He asked me what that was all about and I said I couldn't talk about it. I was talking with the attorneys for the cities and they were asking me questions about the air pollution calculations. I told my boss that it was information the attorneys were asking for and had asked me to keep confidential. He didn't know why I took the call rather than giving it to him. My new boss demanded I tell him what it was about since I was on the clock working for him, so I told him. He was more upset about the fact they had not gone through him to see if it was O.K. to use his staff for their purposes than happy about my being helpful to the "cause." I was surprised. The attorneys were working for the ACC who were funding the RCAA and in my mind, helping them must surely be contractually allowed so I started to think maybe he just didn't like me?

On another occasion my boss mentioned a conflict of interest with my working at RCAA while heading the CASE group and suggested that I consider resigning from CASE. I had always believed that my experience with CASE and all the information I had was an asset to RCAA and that the two groups were fighting the same cause. The only difference between the two was RCAA had funding handed to them while CASE funded itself with citizen donations. Members of the RCAA board were also members of CASE and visa-versa. If RCAA got an idea, they called upon their workforce, the CASE group, to do the job since all they had was a board of directors, a handful of people. I told him I wouldn't even consider resigning from CASE. Even though RCAA provided me with necessary income, I knew I could find another job. RCAA could hire anyone off the street to try to put all their crap in order. But the CASE group, innocent, downtrodden people who were genuinely harmed and hurting, I felt needed someone to give them hope and for whatever reason, they had elected me to do that twice.

Meanwhile, through the RCAA web site and e-mail I was making connections with other groups around the country. Jack, from a group in Chicago called Alliance of Residents Concerned with O'Hare (AReCO) had been fighting the expansion plans piecemealed into O'Hare for a number of years. He was calling the RCAA office often. Jack had a lot of information he shared with me, and likewise, I shared what our group was doing. He was an activist like myself, totally bent on putting a dent into the aviation industries expansionist ideology, although at the time, I called it revenge for ruining my life. Jack told me about a number of other groups from around the country who had been in contact with him. I was also receiving messages from a Friends of the Earth (FOE) Europe group called "The Right Price for Air Travel Campaign" headed by Paul deClerek. Janette Barros in Australia fighting Kingsford Smith Airport expansion was in contact with RCAA through the web page and e-mail. Another group in Mexico was calling.

The European campaign backed by Friends of the Earth Europe reported that a group of protestors in Manchester had built tree houses and underground tunnels where they installed iron gates. They were living in the tree houses and periodically chaining themselves to the gates to stop the bulldozers from plowing down a forest to build a runway. People were bringing them food until razor wire fences were put up by the airport personnel. Eventually the protestors were beaten with clubs and dragged off to jail in a night raid. And progress continues on.

I talked to the local media about this event and they ran an article with the title paraphrased; Local activist (me) supports (wild) civil disobedience (protests) in Manchester. Not quite what I had said, but this is how these things get translated into ink and paper.

Again, my boss was less than happy about my crazy office antics. Being interviewed by the local paper apparently was not in my job description. Neither was spending funds making long distance calls to Jack. He demanded I remove everything about the CASE group from the office and stop my grassroots activism. He wanted the two groups separated. If the activists wanted to use the copier for the 'cause' they could pay for them unless they were somehow for the benefit of RCAA.

Everything came to a head one day when Greg, the water expert who was then working for RCAA, called and asked to be paid for some consulting work he had done. RCAA owed him $1,000.00 and by now, it was long past due. I called a board member and asked him what to do since my boss was unavailable. He asked me to look up the minutes where the board had approved the expenditure. I found them, an approval of the work had been signed by the board members predating my current boss, and this board member came and picked them up. When my boss returned I told him about Greg's request but he refused to write Greg a check even though I assured him the now missing minutes had approved the expenditure. He claimed he knew nothing of the agreement and was fairly certain that hiring a consultant was contrary to the contract RCAA had with the cities.

Greg, an expert who CASE regularly relied upon, needed at least half the money right away. The board member assured me he would clear everything up at the next RCAA board meeting in a few days and would let my boss know it was not contrary to the agreement with the cities.

The day of the board meeting my boss asked me not to attend. It would be executive session and they wouldn't be recording minutes. I again asked about the check for Greg as he had continued to call and was now indicating he would never work for any of us in the future unless this were immediately cleared up. I assured Greg I would do my best. My boss told me that the board member and minutes were not going to be back in town and they had no intention of taking up the matter, no plans to pay Greg and there were other pressing issues to talk about. I told him that if they weren't going to pay Greg, CASE would have to. He cautioned that we had better not. I said that Greg is going to quit altogether if we don't'. He said that would not be his problem since he was sure RCAA should have never got involved with hiring him in the first place and questioned me on what value if any his work had on issues in RCAA's charge. I then asked if my termination would be on the agenda if CASE cut him a check, especially in light of this current disagreement. He said he was not going to answer that. I guessed, by the disapproving look on his face that it was. He then left the office to return sometime later for the meeting. I called Pat and a few other CASE board members to find out whether there would be a majority approving the payment for Greg, which received a welcomed response. I assured them we would be paid back once the matter was cleared up. I then wrote out my resignation and left it on the table of the board room. The RCAA board voted to accept it.

Greg is probably one of the most valuable assets the CASE group has had over the years. Through Waste Action Project, he has been involved in discovery of airport wastewater problems that led to a lawsuit being filed by CASE which documented over 100 violations of the permit and clean water act. The legal team who sued on behalf of CASE, managed to secure access for Greg to periodically inspect airport wastewater facilities which has led to stronger National Pollutant Discharge Elimination System (NPDES) permit requirements, one of the best in the country.

Minnie is the one who actually found Greg long before I joined her group of three. Although the original meeting where she had planned to meet Greg was to include the same RCAA board member who let me down, he never showed up. He was also going to try and get funding for Greg from the cities. That never happened either. Minnie ended up paying Greg thousands out of her own pocket even though Greg would be formally adopted by RCAA and CASE shortly thereafter. Minnie's efforts would never be properly recognized or reimbursed. I think everyone in CASE would agree that Minnie's finding Greg was one of the best things that ever happened to our group and the local water resources.

After about a week, I asked some of our CASE board members to meet with RCAA. I was sure I could flush out some monkey business. By this time the whole matter had been cleared up and RCAA had paid the additional $500.00 they owed Greg which should have necessitated a refund of $500.00 to CASE. I believed my boss had been trying to get rid of either me or Greg, or maybe both and I wanted the CASE board to see and hear for themselves what had happened. I pointed out the obvious double standard in RCAA wanting CASE matters out of their office while wanting CASE members to be their volunteer staff to stuff envelopes, make phone calls or be the stars of their next news story. My CASE board members, trusting sheep that they are, didn't see a problem with RCAA working with us on their terms. If they needed us, we would be there, if they wanted to shun us, we would be duly shunned.

While the RCAA board were acting like they didn't know what I was talking about, the CASE board were looking at me like I was the enemy. I flatly asked my former boss for our $500.00 dollars back. He refused to discuss it. He said it was our choice to pay Greg. He hadn't asked us to get involved in their business.

We had voluntarily paid Greg and the CASE board thought it was a good idea when I asked them and still thought it was a good idea now. I couldn't win. These trusting sheep would never even consider that one of their own could do anything that might hurt us or the cause. I wasn't going to convince them there was a problem without first making them hardened and cynical, like me. I didn't want that. Neither would they. They were happy to give up their citizen donations, once to pay RCAA through the ACC and again, to pay RCAA's bills for them. They didn't care. They wanted a happy ending. So be it. Baaaaaa, baaaaaa.

It's bad enough that none of the agencies who are supposed to protect us are on our side, at times, *we're* not even on our side! So often when it might have made a critical difference and maybe brought about a turning point in our battle, we were let down, sometimes by each other, or sidetracked by our own inabilities to agree on what to do next. Personalities get in the way, some are using their tenure at these various organizations to climb into a political career and don't really care about the 'cause.'

On occasion, I have asked RCAA to approve various things the CASE group couldn't easily afford. They were not interested in diverting any of their funds from the basic task of educating everyone through their newsletter. During the three days when aviation was suspended for the national crisis just after 9/11/01, I found a consulting firm who was willing to put air pollution monitors around the airport for $1,800.00. The ACC cities and RCAA refused to help fund it. I thought it would be a great comparative tool to have since the airport has claimed for years that the rates of NO2, benzene and formaldehyde and other cancer causing emissions in our neighborhoods would be the same without the airport there.

Then there is that bargain deal with the air pollution model the FAA offered to the cities but would not extend to me. Maybe it is because the FAA knew the cities wouldn't buy it. I begged the consultant who pulled apart the intersection carbon monoxide to look into the EDMS model data input and tried to convince the ACC to allow it but they were unwilling to do so. People often thought attorneys the ACC had hired were brought in to obtain mitigation for the cities rather than victory for the residents. Who knows what the truth is, but for our group, we could never seem to agree on what was going on, which way it should go or how we should get somewhere from here.

For every one of nearly 100 members who would regularly attend our monthly meetings, there were 100 little battles waging. I would ask people if they could work on just this issue or that, but everyone was busy working on their own issue. Whether its kerosene odors in the neighborhood, calling the hotline constantly about noise, soot on patios, run-ups, unusual flight paths, water problems, old lawsuits, property losses, noise in schools, you name it, we had someone working on it. But anything together?

Agencies weren't watching over us, laws weren't protecting us, government wasn't validating our complaints, cities weren't helping us and we often weren't supporting ourselves.

ACC's case against the Port, PSRC and FAA was lost. The tape of the hearing which had no discussion of the illegal conformity determination the attorneys had discussed in their comments and brief, prefaced their argument for reconsideration with an admission by the attorney representing us that the region ***needed*** the runway. Hog wash.

Even though we still had the air quality study and the Army Corps wetland delineation to be completed, our group was losing ground and losing hope.

I truly believed if you could get a bunch of people all working on the same thing, it could make a difference. During my last days at RCAA and the networking I was now involved in with a number of other groups in the US and abroad, I believed putting together a national coalition might accomplish that. If we got all the leaders of groups around the country together, and I was finding there were many of them, tapped into their respective experts via the internet, and went after the industry on a national level, maybe we could gain respect and recognition for our issues.

It was late summer 1997 and Paul De Clerek from the European campaign wanted to visit with us. Helen, a gracious hostess for political meetings and one of our CASE board members, cookie contributor and fundraising managers offered to supply him with a room in her gorgeous home on Miller Creek in Normandy Park. He stayed for several days and we took him around and explained what has happened so far. He met with several members of our respective groups, discussed strategy, and then left completely unimpressed to visit other groups in the US. I didn't hear from him again. After a few years of vigorous work, aggressive activism and many reports, Friends of the Earth Europe dissolved the "Right Price For Air Travel Campaign" and went on to other matters.

Although Paul was not very impressed by our efforts, I believed our group had the most sophisticated four pronged attack plan imaginable. We had amassed a multi-million dollar legal action against the runway plan. We had a newsletter going out to thousands of people each quarter detailing the events, how to get involved, where to donate time, energy and resources. We had experts in every field to challenge the assumptions and conclusions of the EIS. We had a large citizen group who protested the process at every turn. Money, the law, experts and activists…How could we lose? In retrospect, I suppose the better question would be how could we win?

Chapter 16

US-CAW
Citizens Aviation Watch Inc.

National Resources Defense Council (NRDC) had published a report "Flying Off Course" in October 1996 documenting air, water and noise pollution problems at the nation's airports. This was the most comprehensive independent study of airport emissions that I had seen up to this point. In this report they had compared several airports in the US with major polluters in their respective districts and found that airports were among the top industrial emission sources along with refineries, incinerators, steel mills, the worst in our nation. LaGuardia in New York, Boston Logan, O'Hare among others were analyzed. NRDC's compilation of jet emission data using the same old EDMS model produced results that were similar to other independent studies and far different from the airport EIS. Ozone precursors, nitrogen oxides and hydrocarbons were analyzed.

They had also reported that these same airports had problems with eliminating de-icing fluids, and less than best practice responses to spills and leaks that were producing a large amount of toxic wastewater problems in nearby creeks and water bodies.

It was through Jack in Chicago that I learned about the NRDC report. He had provided information to the investigative team at NRDC and received several copies of their report, one of which he mailed to me. Jack and I were in constant contact through e-mail discussing an upcoming legal action by NRDC on airport wastewater. Through his contacts, I was in touch with someone named Steve who lived in Baltimore.

Steve had moved into his home and over the course of some years living near Baltimore Washington International Airport, (BWI) noticed the airport had begun to conduct nighttime jet engine run-ups. This noise was waking him up. People who have tried to do something about noise have been worn out by the endless dead ends. Noise complaint lines keep the problem internal, lack of local government involvement leaves people with nowhere else to turn. Residents have resigned themselves to just live with it. But Steve expected to be able to sleep through the night and he took his concerns to the airport personnel. They let him know that they pretty much could care less about him. They were running an airport. They laughed at his request and explained that peaceful sleep, somehow a luxury, was not in their purview. Not knowing Steve well at this time that we began our communication, I pretty much took this as the normal response, felt bad for him, but told him there was probably nothing he could do about it. This was not acceptable to Steve at all. He would launch a systematic plan meant to make those who had expressed such little concern, completely and thoroughly sorry they had done so.

Steve is not an average guy. He holds an important non elected position with the United States Government. His sleep was important to him and his work, and actually, for us all. He is well educated as are many of the people airports wish to brand as morons who moved into the problems. Truth is, airports are moving themselves into communities more and more every year, but people don't get this side of the story. BWI moved their run-ups at 1:30 a.m. every night into Steve's sleep in the mid 1990's without any advance warning.

Steve got involved with the local activist group and pretty soon, was making suggestions for courses of action for his group of seniors. Although not an easy task, he was trying to drum up some real military Tai Chi zeal from his group and had initially contacted me to learn more about our local successes. I suggested protests.

The European campaign was holding "Action Days on Aviation." Groups from all over Europe were engaged in very bold protests like sitting on a plane in the Netherlands. For my contribution to the action day, I asked my group if they were willing to participate in a protest at the airport. My group was horrified. Although they thought it was a great idea and might even make the front page of the European newsletter, there was no way they were going risk getting arrested. My alternative suggestion that we peacefully hand out flyers inside the terminal was accepted. My radical members wanted confirmation that we wouldn't be arrested so I secured written permission from the Port Police and showed it to them. There was only one problem, nobody wanted to go. After the last two reluctant protest volunteers came up with 'other plan' excuses the night before, I ended up going by myself. While I was standing handing out flyers, Gina Marie Lindsey, the acting Aviation Director walked by, turned and said hello to me by name. I had never met her but she knew me. I thought that was odd. Maybe she had seen me at one of the hearings. I gave her a US-CAW flier. Jack and & I had written the flier and it covered air, noise and water pollution problems at various airports. At a meeting not too long after this she said we should go have coffee and talk sometime. I said sure.

I took Arlene and we met with her at Starbucks where she treated us to coffee. I explained to her that the emissions at Sea-Tac are causing cancer and other health problems in our community. She believed that if it were as bad as we claimed, she would know about it. Her staff would have told her. She also thought the local air agencies would fine them or shut down the airport if it were as bad as we claimed. We explained how and why airports are exempt from this type of regulation. Arlene and I appealed to her as a mother with our concerns for our children growing up in this kind of an environment.

I believed her when she told us she didn't know it was as bad as we said and I wasn't nearly as angry at her as I thought I would be. I had pictured her as a heartless villain bent on the destruction of thousands of lives. But for the moment, I saw her as a real person, who had climbed to the top of her field, a major success for any woman, and she seemed sincere in her desire to get to the bottom of it. She never got back to us. Steve believed she knew about the problems beforehand and never intended to do anything.

My approach to appeal to people's conscience was a little too soft-soap for Steve. Awareness raising was not his forte. Although I didn't have too many positive results to share with him, I would learn he didn't need my help or advice. He had ways of attacking big problems head on with plenty of training to do so.

Steve had found out that the Sawmill creek near BWI was carrying glycol contamination from BWI's storm drains. At the same time the governor of Maryland was publicly hailing the creek restoration program as a wonderful success, Steve and his activist friends were videotaping a 4' head of de-icing foam on the creek, near a wellhead for drinking water serving Anne Arundel County residents. This creek and glycol contamination at O'Hare, Sea-Tac and BWI became the subject of a radio broadcast, and subsequently, a Clean Water Act lawsuit by Natural Resources Defense Council (NRDC).

As discovery progressed and the airport tried to defend themselves against it using much less than valid arguments, the Department of Justice intervened. They warned that if NRDC didn't take a settlement agreement they would just change the law. Under this pressure, NRDC settled requiring BWI to install some kind of better collection container where wastewater could be retained and then trucked to a treatment facility. The new system, according to Steve, would be expensive but not provide 100% retention. Sometime during this process, the trees behind his house were set on fire. On another occasion, Steve was driving home one night and was shot at. Nobody knows what involvement the airport had, no suspects were ever caught. Is it coincidental or malicious? One incident, maybe, but two? Steve realized that if the Department of Justice were getting involved in a little action like this, there was probably no way to ever fight or win in this battle. The stakes are so high, power so entrenched that individuals don't have a chance. He moved. I still wanted to believe that right is might no matter how easily the airport could crush our every attempt.

One CASE activist, tried for two years to get the airport to admit their glycol used for de-icing was entering the creeks since it had been found in random testing. The Port insisted the levels in the creek were not from airport sources because they rarely used it and when they did, runoff is contained and treated in the Industrial Wastewater Treatment (IWS) facility. The most likely source would be residents' use of antifreeze or local car repair shops. Through diligence and perseverance she finally obtained Port documents revealing glycol is used 280 days out of the year and other documents that said the IWS system is not able to treat glycol which was a direct contradiction of the Port's claims. When you put all the pieces of the puzzle together, you find out untreated antifreeze is infiltrating the creeks 280 days a year. But they make it so difficult to get to the bottom of anything. It takes years of full time work, research techniques have to be finely honed talents. In her research, she also found out the creeks contained fecal coliform the airport insisted was from bird droppings washing off rooftops during rainstorms. But when the fecal coliform was tested it was found to be human and because of a unique additive also found, the likely source became the washing of the biffy tanks (airline toilets) near the headwaters of Des Moines Creek next to airport property.

Placing blame on anything and anybody but airport operations is typical and expected. They have made a science out of the run-around and the blame game. They tell you to call Ecology for air who they know won't do anything because the law doesn't allow it. They tell you to call their noise line for complaints and that information never goes anywhere. They tell you to call PSCAA for dust which they don't regulate at the airport. They tell you to call EPA about the creeks which they have delegated responsibility to the state to regulate. They blame the soot on tires and wood burning stoves. They blame the noise problem on homeowners for moving to the area. The airport blames residents' use of antifreeze and birds for problems in the creeks, drivers for the emission problems at the airport and so on. While everyone is expending all their extra income and time running after their tails trying to get to the bottom of it all, airport bad guys are collecting their salary. Hardly seems fair.

Meanwhile, the CO monitoring was finding little validation for the predicted air quality violations from cars. Probably the worst hot-spot along the curb front for passenger pick up and drop off, which might have produced dramatic results if the airport had not blocked the placement of monitors during the busy holiday period, was still slightly below the federal standard and no mitigation was required. PSCAA wrote the high carbon monoxide figure from the Delta Departure Gate had been found by using methods deemed unacceptable according to EPA standards. Testing for carbon monoxide near the jet sources was not done during the study.

The air quality team had issued a draft of their preliminary report on the permanent monitors for NO2 and particulate. The rates were not significant at the northeast particulate monitor. It was not directly under the flight path of arriving and departing planes and still no hauling of dirt for the third runway had been conducted. The south monitor, directly under the flight path in Tyee Golf Course where Ecology had previously predicted violations of the federal standard had the nephelometer which captured light disturbance and was to be compared to a monitor which took readings once every six days. The graph type of readout, similar to an EKG in appearance, required an analysis that compared it to the monitor on days they both operated to estimate rates for the days in between. This was delayed until there was very little money left for further analysis. I also ran out of time during this period to understand how to decipher the graph. Normally I would be pulling it apart and arguing with the staff. It's easier to read hieroglyphics than to understand this thing. I kicked myself for not finding out more before placement was decided. The permanent particulate monitor should have been placed under the jets at Tyee, not the other way around. I now believe this was a purposeful tact. Ecology knew what they were doing.

Although the initial findings from the badge samplers had created quite a stir, the NO2 draft report indicated the rates were below the annual federal standard of .053 with the annual result for the northeast monitor the higher of the two at .021. The draft did mention something interesting however. They decided to shuffle the data and use the lowest captured wind speed to determine the source. During this time when the air traveled past the south Tyee monitor in a northeasterly direction over the runways, toward the northeast monitor at Riverton Heights, the Tyee monitor registered .017 and the Riverton monitor registered .040. Similarly, when the wind was the opposite direction, the same scenario occurred. This meant there was a significant source of NO in between the two monitors. But the narrative summarized that at this time, it is difficult to ascertain the source or the magnitude of the source… more studies would be needed. There is only one thing in between the two, the stinking airport. It doesn't take a rocket scientist to see it's the airport. The annual rate was higher than historical Beacon Hill rates which were the highest in the county when the monitoring van sampled four years earlier. I surmised it might be possible that the two airports, Sea-Tac and Boeing Field, both in line with Beacon Hill from the southwest, could be the source of the Beacon Hill rates. They are, after all, the largest producer of NO of any other sources in the county, even the FAA admitted that in the EIS. But the air regulatory agencies didn't see it, or did they? I don't know how or why it could happen, but I also suspect aircraft operations might have been altered during the testing but I will never be able to confirm this.

It was early in 1998 and the national group wanted to start a coalition. We had an initial conference call which included Jack in Chicago, who would be elected President of the newly founded group, Dr. Frans Verhaagen, an environmental sociologist from New York who heads the group Sane Aviation for Everyone (SAFE), Steve representing the BWI group, two representatives from Denver, one an acoustical engineer, Dick from Minneapolis, Don from Washington DC, Pam from New Jersey, Jerry of the El Toro group in California, others and myself, who was more of a moderator than the organizer during the call.

After about 10 minutes of bantering about names for the organization we agreed on US Citizens Aviation Watch (US-CAW). One of the members dropped out almost immediately because she thought we might be sued by Citizen Watch Company for using their name.

We would collect seed money from each group to start up a web site, hire experts if necessary and push for legislation in DC. Our motto; "Advocating an equitable, accountable and sustainable aviation industry", reflects the three major problems with the industry we all agreed need attention. We wanted to address the subsidies, tax breaks, power, governance structure and privileges the aviation industry enjoys that no other industry receives. They should pay their way as any business. They should also charge the right price for air travel which covers the damage the industry causes to the environment and local communities. These costs and losses are presently being ignored. If it is 2.95 billion just for Sea-Tac, (which does not include anything for health care or premature deaths due to noise and jet emissions, costs to local schools or costs from the other two runways) national costs might be as much as 100 billion considering 50 busy airports.

Since the industry is not regulated, monitored or controlled like all other industry, it is not accountable to the usual policing that protects the public and environment from destructive effects. Presently, they are only accountable to themselves.

The industry is not sustainable and with the intensive use of non-renewable resources aviation demands, its present irresponsible behavior is unjustifiable. Irresponsible in the sense that there are so many short hop flights each day that can be accommodated by alternative modes of transportation, planes are not always full, the ticket price doesn't reflect the real cost of doing business, making air travel more desirable for people who could not otherwise afford it which drives up demand, demand that is contrived or forced rather than necessary. Peak hour push is likely behind many airport expansion plans, but planners won't admit it. Recently in Philadelphia, one of the PHL CAW members who frequently blogs on Aviation Watch, wrote to me that their EIS used the foggy delays for their purpose and need for expansion.

Recent justification for expansion of Heathrow, where you would expect foggy delays might really exist, included the argument that all the poor should be able to fly. If you fight against this purpose and need, then I suppose you might be branded as an elitist or unkind toward the poor, a cruel position. Maybe they are using no frills pavement to justify the lower ticket price. Maybe while you ruin whole cities, make one hundred thousand people sick to death from noise and fumes, it can be justified because it is a humanitarian effort to help the poor? At least one EU economist has questioned this alleged need by pointing out things that nobody has thought about like, hey, can they afford to go on a vacation? Where will they go? Maybe it's because doing something for the poor sounds a lot better on paper than building a runway for the rich, which likely will hurt only the poor.

Our newly founded US-CAW group decided to oppose a bill sponsored by a senator from Arizona called Air 21. This bill would funnel billions into the aviation industry over the course of 20 years, not for mitigation, nothing for residents, solely to aid in expansion programs.

As a result of our new efforts and networking with other groups, Noise Pollution Clearing House invited activists to a conference in NY in November 1999. I took the train from Seattle to New York. The Empire Builder which runs from Seattle to Chicago was a very enjoyable ride. Although it took two days, it gave me time to read, relax and enjoy the scenery. I formed a couple of conclusions on the way. First, if you take Montana out of the way, the trip would be a day shorter. Second, if the tracks were upgraded so the trains could travel above 85 mph, it would take a day and a half even with Montana in the way. There were very few people on the train and those that were there I engaged in conversation every chance I had. I found out there are some people who frequently use the rail system. It's roomy, the seats are comfortable, they have a snack bar, show movies at night, serve liquor, have power outlets at every seat, showers, sleeper cars and even a nice restaurant car with great food. One young man from Europe was on a countrywide excursion where he could stop in any city, stay for awhile, hop back on and travel anywhere he wanted for a month for a minimal fee. He told me trains in Europe are the preferred mode of travel and he enjoys them. But the train from Chicago to New York was another story. The Lakeshore Limited runs along a very old stretch of track. It was bumpy, seemed old and packed full of people. I asked several train employees why and they explained there is never enough money in the budget to upgrade. They run on a shoe-string and can barely make costs. There is never a profit. I thought this was an ideal topic to bring up at the conference…nothing for trains, everything for planes.

The conference was held at a beautiful mountain cabin in the Adirondacks. The food was great and the group was enthusiastic. Although we left the conference with many ideas about what should happen next, we failed to follow through on many of these. The list of efforts probably had a person attached to each item. Again, we each had our own area we wanted to focus attention. There is nothing wrong with this, except it makes it difficult to organize a single offensive when everyone is going in 10 different directions. Lobbying for rail funding seemed inappropriate to even bring up.

Jack gave me an environmental impact statement for the Cleveland Hopkins International Airport expansion program to read on the train going home. It was written by the same consulting firm who had written the Sea-Tac EIS. As I began to read through it, I noticed much of the same type of confusing data presentation, inadequate analysis and false assumptions which had permeated ours. There was very little information about air quality but one thing caught my attention. In the letters from community members I read comments that were so similar to our concerns, especially about health and the air quality. An elected official wrote:

"It is conceivable that we will have more planes flying over your homes at lower levels, sending more jet fuel on your homes and out in the air you breathe if we get a tremendous amount of increase in airplane traffic without our concerns being dealt with.

The people who live near the airport, it's been proven, have more health problems then(sic) people who live far away from the airport."[51]

"There are noise problems and pollution problems that must be dealt with to the satisfaction of the people who live nearby.

The economy of northeast Ohio is not dependent solely on the airport, the economy also depends on the relative stability and peace and quiet of people who live in communities like Olmsted Falls and Olmsted Township. And, if communities such as this are not healthy, then the economy is not healthy."[52]

Chapter 17

SDOPH

"The airport and airport-related activities are potentially major sources of air pollution and environmental justice requires that one group of people not benefit at the cost of environmental degradation affecting the quality of life of another group."[53]

The State Department of Public Health (SDOPH) had been pressured by a state senator to survey the zip codes around the airport to see what the cancer statistics might show. After a lengthy letter writing barrage, the SDOPH finally surveyed a 1, 3 and 5 mile radius around the airport for years 1992 through 1995. Unfortunately, many of the cases which might have occurred within the 1 mile corridors of the flight paths to the north and south of the airport were not included in the initial survey. Seventeen hundred homes had been removed by 1995. Still, the statistics were alarming enough to make the lead story on the evening news. Glioblastoma brain tumors in the 1 mile area around the airport were found to be 75% higher than state average, 40% higher in the 3 mile area and dropped down again for the 5 mile area. There were also 211 more cancer cases above expected equal to more than 10% above average, similar to the increase previously modeled by EPA at Midway Airport. These rates were initially compared to the state average:

	Area 1		Area 2		Area 3	
	Observed	Expected	Observed	Expected	Observed	Expected
All Cancer	2,222*	2,011	3,577*	3,319	5,363*	5,096
Leukemia	55	48	89	79	140	122
Glioma	35	25	49	43	65	66
Glioblastoma	21*	12	28	20	33	31

*When we assess the range of statistical variation which we consider normal, we conclude that the number of
54
cases is higher than expected.

Audrey summarized the above tables with the percentages she derived of increase in incidence over state average:

	Area 1	Areas 1 & 2	Areas 1, 2 & 3
All cancer	10.49	7.77	5.24
Leukemia	14.58	12.66	14.75
Glioma	40.00	13.95	-1.53
Glioblastoma	75.00	40.00	6.45

Statistics from Boeing Field were also published which found that 98108 zip code, the community closest to Boeing Field in Georgetown, Washington, had alarming numbers including a 57% higher than average expected asthma rate, 28% higher pneumonia influenza rate, 26% higher respiratory disease rate, 83% higher pregnancy complication, 50% higher infant mortality, genetic diseases, mortality rates 48% higher for all causes of death, 57% higher heart disease, 36% higher cancer death rate and average life expectancy at 70.4 years compared to nearby Seattle at 76.0.

These disease and death rates from both Georgetown and communities near Sea-Tac have been advertised in flyers, protests, newspapers and discussed endlessly with air regulators. The statistics from these two surveys are so alarming, it is amazing to me that people have failed to fall over in shock. It appears that the closer you live to the airport the greater chance you have of developing cancer, especially brain tumors. The SDOPH were compelled from these statistics however, to take a closer look. They assembled a team of community representatives, worked with the King County Department of Public Health and a work plan for discovery was developed.

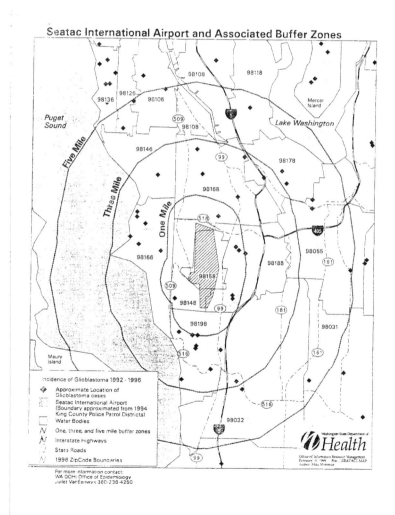

Seatac International Airport and Associated Buffer Zones

The map to the left, developed by the State Department of Public Health in 1999 shows the circles of the one, three and five mile areas surveyed. The circle closest to the airport represents much of what is called the Highline district. To the left of the airport represented as 98158 is the City of Burien at 98166. Directly below is Des Moines at 98198, to the right is city of Sea-Tac in 98188. On the map there is only one dot representing Riverton Heights just to the top and right. This is the neighborhood where Rose's push-pin map had 4 cases of glioblastoma. Riverton Heights was bought out before the survey dates of 1992 to 1995. To the south, there were eventually 17 cases of glioblastoma found in 98198 with a population of only 22,000 but the map shows only 8 cases. I don't know where the other 9 cases went.

In 1998, 21 cases in the one mile area were discovered in zip code data by SDOPH. Now on the map from 1999, there are only 6 in that same circle for years 1992 to 1996. There should be more with another year added, not 15 less. To the north and south in the flight path, thousands of people had been removed, yet a small sampling of households revealed another 34 brain cancer cases. These would appear in 98168 and 98198 where I see only 10 in the three mile area. One can only wonder if the airport finally bought these people out after 20 years of waiting after the second runway was added in 1973 to scatter the numbers of illnesses. Only one case was found worthy to be added to the survey but the totals do not nearly reflect the cumulative data of the original numbers with added cases found through additional surveys. Data was subsequently manipulated, skewed, diluted and downplayed and suddenly 1992 became the only year with higher than average numbers. Instead of comparing rates to state average, the survey compared to King County with 3 airports and the highest illness rates in the state. Zip code 98198 was somehow dropped from the analysis. Significantly higher disease rates were later also dropped from the analysis.

Ideally, the data collection should come from the flight paths and downwind communities which could be represented by a more oval shaped circle

Audrey, Rose, Arlene and Dr. Hansa were some of the people invited to the community representative meetings with the health department. I had asked to be on the committee but was not included. That was fine with me since I was a bit busy. I had remarried. My new husband lived to the west of the airport, an upwind area with healthy plants, but nonetheless, affected. This came about as a result of a suggestion once again from Pat to enlist my CASE secretary Dave as a date (my first in 22 years). This brought about a new marriage, new baby, new son (Dave had sole custody of a son from a previous relationship), moving, new schools, new job, starting my life entirely over once again. Funny how I sat next to Dave for two years at CASE meetings and never noticed what a great guy he is until Pat helped me see it.

The community representatives did give me copies of the subsequent reports. In one of them I noticed the average incidence of glioblastoma brain tumors in King County was 3 in 100,000 person population[55] which initially would have included the Sea-Tac communities. Originally the SDOPH had compared the Sea-Tac rates to state rates at 2.7 per 100,000 and found cases in the one mile area to be 75% higher than average. Since there were approximately 98,000 people living in the area of study, 33 divided by the four years is eight per year, nearly triple the state rate, well above 75% higher. One of the CASE activists wrote to the National Brain Tumor Foundation who sent a booklet "Central Brain Tumor Registry of the United States" (CBTR) which also had the glioblastoma brain tumor incidence of occurrence at 3 per 100,000 (an average broken down by age, sex and race).[56] People under 60, women and people other than white are less likely to develop them. We had a high number of women under 60 in the Sea-Tac communities develop glioblastoma which is out of the norm according to the CBTR. I wondered if it was because women stayed at home while men worked away from the airport pollution?

Over the next couple of years, the SDOPH work plan was expanded to include a search of available information on the relationship between these brain tumors and types of emissions present from airport sources which might be a contributor. Formaldehyde is suspected to cause brain tumors. Pathologists and embalmers who work with formaldehyde have reported higher than average rates. Formaldehyde levels 47 times higher than the ASIL had been measured near the neighborhoods around the airport by MFG. Nearly 63 tons per year is released at Midway Airport in Chicago, an amount a senior scientist at EPA called a 'mind blower.' SDOPH mentioned Dr. Olin's study in their summary and many other reports discussing a relationship of certain chemicals including vinyl chloride, PAH and nitrous compounds to brain tumors. But yet, they were unable to determine any relationship between the airport emissions and brain tumors during their study of Sea-Tac.

As the search continued and more illnesses were added the list, they found that lung cancer rates were 19% higher than county levels. Larynx and esophagus cancers were also elevated. There are a dozen chemicals present in jet exhaust that are lung and throat irritants.

But more studies would be needed…of course. This time, more research would be needed as well since the causal relationship between chemical and cancer incidence was eluding the SDOPH. Factors to convert emissions into cancer risk estimates exist and on more than one occasion I suggested they develop a risk analysis using MFG and modeling. This never happened. However, discussion of air monitoring began. The community group wanted our area compared to another area such as Shoreline without industrial sources while the SDOPH along with King County wanted Beacon Hill. As I have discussed earlier, Beacon Hill is downwind from Georgetown industrial processes, near two freeways and under the flight path of three airports, and frequently downwind from both Sea-Tac and Boeing Field emissions. Actually, there would be no harm in having just Sea-Tac air toxics measured for risk analysis. But I realize once they have the data, there would be a rush to compare it to another polluted area and call it good. They then dispel and ignore the results and carry on business as usual.

People who had responded to questionnaires sent out to a number of homeowners who had been removed from the flight paths had a very low response rate. The majority who responded and reported cancer were either diagnosed before 1992 or after 1995. Only one additional case of brain cancer was added as a result of surveying a small portion of the thousands of people who had been removed even though 34 brain tumors were reported. Ten were diagnosed before 1992 and eight after 1996. Sixteen needed investigation but I cannot find the results of the investigation. Fifteen which might have been added are not discussed further. Questionnaires sent to businesses at and adjacent to the airport had such a low response rate they were dismissed due to lack of a better sampling. I am including parts of a letter originally addressed to 20/20 from one airport worker who did respond. It gives an inside look at what went on with the businesses:

"My name is Mark Beem, I'm a driver for Emery Worldwide at Sea-Tac Airport, Seattle, Washington. In Nov. of 1999, I was diagnosed with a melanoma on my left leg. Since then I have had two surgeries, the most recent being a groin dissection to remove all of the lymph nodes in my left groin area. I am presently on medical leave from work and soon will have the area radiated and then receive 30 days of Interferon. My surgeon's diagnosis is that it's a 50/50 chance that I will live another five years. I am only the latest casualty at Emery Worldwide in what has been an unbelievable number of health problems (see attached copy.) The numbers are staggering considering Emery has only approximately 70 to 80 long term employees. I believe our health problems are caused by our work location which is adjacent to the runways on the northeast side of Sea-Tac Airport. Considering the southwest prevailing wind, we are in the worst location for exposure to the pollution from the aircraft that take off to the south approximately 60% of the time."

"Concerned residents of the Sea-Tac Airport area, did a health Survey that was published on February 5, 1999. As part of the Survey, questionnaires were sent by WDOH([4]) to 111 businesses located around the perimeter of the runways at Sea-Tac Airport (on POS[5] property) in November of 1998. The employers were asked to pass these questionnaires out to all of their employees. The questionnaire asked for information regarding incidences of cancer among employees from 1985 to 1998. The WDOH received responses from only 14 businesses – of those, only three reported known cases of cancer. I question, would there have been a better response rate had the questionnaires been sent directly to the employees to be returned to the WDOH rather than through the employers? I wonder how many of the questionnaires even got into the hands of the employees. I also wonder how many of the employees cared to pass such personal information on to their employers. I, as an employee of Emery Worldwide, did not receive a questionnaire, nor do I know of anyone else who received one."

"I do know that Delta Airlines moved 150 reservationists out of a building near the tarmac in 1993. Their vice president told three employee groups that they were relocating them because they were 'not in a healthy environment.' Many of the reservationists were suffering from illnesses they suspected were from airport pollution. Some were chemically poisoned with benzene in their blood. There were cases of breast, thyroid, and lung cancer. Six of the women had miscarriages in a three-year period. One of the women employees had her first child die of bone cancer at age two or three. There was

---

[4] Authors note: Acronym WDOH is the same as SDOPH, Washington Department of Public Health
[5] Port of Seattle

a lawsuit and as part of the settlement, the employees were asked not to talk about it."

I had heard of the Delta reservationists' health problems years earlier when I spoke with one former employee. She had not been included in the action because her symptoms had shown up after the case was started so she freely shared information. Besides telling me they all tested positive for benzene in their blood, which she said never goes away, she was also struggling with memory loss. When I called her some time later to find out the results of the cases and get updated on health outcomes for the employees, she didn't remember who I was or know what I was talking about. I am not sure if this was an additional aspect of the cases hush order extended to her or if her memory loss was worse.

I also wrote to 20/20 as US-CAW/Mothers Against Airport Pollution (MAAP) asking them to investigate the high numbers of illnesses around the nation's airports. I cited the report from NRDC which said pollution levels at airports are comparable to steel mills and refineries, sent our statistics and others supplied by various groups writing to Jack in Chicago. As far as I know, Mark never heard back from 20/20 and neither did US-CAW.

Mark however, compiled the following statistics on his co-workers and included this with his letter:

NAME	AGE	SERVICE	ILLNESS	ADDITIONAL INFORMATION
Ray Monson	40	3 years	*heart attack	Died in 1992
Ken Rohr	60	8 years	*heart attack	Retired in 1996 – died in 1998
John Litchfield	60	32 years	Brain tumor	A benign tumor in forehead
George Batman	45	1 year	Cancer	Died in 1990
Walt Jones	56	10 years	Cancer	Had a colostomy in 1998

Janet Ude	45	10 years	Cancer	Left in 1990
E. J. Moe	65	35 years	Cancer	Retired in 1990-died 3 months later
Jim Macek	48	20 years	Cancer	Had prostate surgery-still working
Jerry Smith	47	25 years	Cancer	On medical leave for prostate cancer
Jack Hill	53	11 years	cancer	Had prostate surgery-still working
Gary Cave	63	11 years	Cancer	Leukemia-retired
Mark Beem	46	24 years	Cancer	Melanoma-on medical leave
Robert Jewell	61	25 years	Cancer	Brain tumor-had surgery 4 yrs ago
Ed Davis	40	4 years	Cancer	Died in 96 of glioblastoma
Brook Jones	48	20 years	Cancer	Died in 89 of glioblastoma
Larry Neff	51	11 years	Cancer	On leave for glioblastoma
Tom Hill	49	25 years	Lupus	On medical leave

When I reviewed Mark's letter for my book I tried to local him and ended up talking to his mother. She told me Mark had died at age 47 of the melanoma which had started in his leg. He had suffered terribly and went through some rough treatments to try to be cured. He had children he left behind and the costs and losses involved with his leave from work put a terrible strain on him and his family. These kinds of human tragedies could have been avoided if the Port would have ever heeded the warnings from study after study. The Delta reservationists' removal should have sent a clear signal to everyone in the area that far more needed to be done than closing just one office.

Working with the national group, I had gathered information from a number of different communities. I found our problems and concerns about emissions and cancer rates are not unique. Fact is, nobody is putting all of this together. Each is being studied in isolation to the respective facility. But these are all the same planes hopping around all over the world so logically, the problems would be similar.

Boston:
> "All over the country, neighbors of airports voice the same complaints. Noise is at the top of the list, followed closely by unhealthy fumes. Tales of weird, sickening, or choking fumes abound. Mary Ellen Welch, who lives adjacent to Boston Logan International in East Boston, says that when the wind is right, stepping out her front door is like 'walking into a vat of kerosene.'
>
> Many people living near airports complain of respiratory problems: burning lungs, breathing difficulty, more frequent attacks of asthma and allergies. They also tell of increased local occurrences of cancer."[57]

Birmingham:
> "Metro Birmingham Alabama offers some of the best health care available, yet its eastern area suffers high rates of serious illnesses such as cancer, stroke and heart attack. The Birmingham International Airport is located in the eastern area of Birmingham. These are the same communities that have been most severely impacted by aviation pollution through the years. Woodlawn and Roebuck, in particular, sit at the end of runways. Health care professionals, community leaders and residents are organizing to find out what's wrong and how to fix it."[58]

Chicago:
> "The new study, released March 21, finds that overall cancer rates in the area near O'Hare are 28 percent higher than the state average, and that jet engine emissions at O'Hare are at least partially responsible. The study further finds

that in the 10-mile area around the airport there are clearly demonstrated cancer "hot-spots" along flight paths that are 33 to 50 percent higher than the overall local area and up to 100 percent higher than the state average."[59]

Australia:

"'Benzene and toluene (similarly dangerous) are created during the incomplete high temperature combustion process in a jet engine...The problem is most prevalent during landing operations as the jet engines are operating outside their design operating range. The benzene, together with excess fuel and other combustion products, are distributed in the air immediately over residential populations'... Benzpyrenes were also a concern. Professor Ken Bradstock, Clinical Associate Professor of Medicine at Westmead hospital's Haematology Department said: 'aircraft engines emit a variety of hydrocarbon by-products, many of which are carcinogenic. The best studied of these is a compound called 3,4 benzpyrene which is a compound which contains a number of benzene rings...Benzpyrene and closely related chemical derivatives are classically described carcinogens. There is an extensive literature going back 20 years...They are capable of producing tumours in laboratory animals at doses of millionths of a gram...there is no safe level of exposure to polycyclic aromatics, particularly compounds like 3,4 benzpyrene'...According to the submission from the Medical Board of the Royal Prince Alfred Hospital and the Central Sydney Area Health Board: 'The most carcinogenic of the substances involved in jet fuel usage are the benzpyrene emissions, in particular the soot from jet fuel is highly carcinogenic in animal experimentations. Jet exhaust provides 2-4 mg of carcinogenic benzopyrenes per minute...This means the release each year of up to 2 kilograms of benzpyrenes onto suburbs near the airport. Professor Bradstock, said 'logic' suggested that such levels of exposure over decades 'would inevitably translate into an excess of deaths from lung and other cancers. Benzpyrenes have been found in soil, vegetation and snow around airports, and in water supplies subjected to jet fuel emission. They are not significantly biodegradable. Levels have remained high in water samples even six months after contamination. The Journal of Epidemiology and Community Health reported in April 1997 on research by the University of Birmingham Medical School which found that children born near sources of atmospheric pollution, including major airports, are up to 20% more likely to die of leukemia and solid tumor (nonblood) cancers before they reach adulthood."[60]

Oakland, a risk analysis found:

"These analyses indicate that off-site health impacts of the Project are significant and would increase the incidence of cancer and respiratory disease in residential neighborhoods around the airport and among employees at the airport itself. The highest exposures would occur in residential areas in Alameda in the southeast section of Bay Farm Island, in residential areas on both sides of 98th Street adjacent to I-880 in Oakland, and north of the San Leandro Marina. The maximum incremental cancer risk in 2010 due to the Project in these locations is 22 in one million and exceeds the significance threshold of 10 in one million by over a factor of two. The maximum incremental noncancer hazard index in 2010 due to the Project is 5 and exceeds the significance threshold of 1 by a factor of 5.

The project would also increase the risk of cancer and noncancer diseases to workers within the MOIA[6]. The maximum exposures would occur north of Runway 29 along a service road in the North Airport. The maximum incremental cancer risk at this location is 16.9 in one million and the maximum chronic noncarcinogenic hazard index is

---

[6] MOIA may be an acronym for the airport Maintenance and Operations Area

28.2 both of which exceed significance thresholds by large margins. Workers within the terminals would also receive significant exposures. The increase in cancer risk among workers within the terminals would be 10.5 in one million and the increase in chronic noncancer risk would be 16.4.

These estimates substantially underestimate the actual health risks posed by the Project because most of the toxic emissions were omitted due to the lack of adequate information in the FEIR[7] and time constraints. The health risks calculated here are only those due to exhaust emissions from aircraft and associated ground support equipment. There are numerous additional sources of toxic emissions at airports, including the exhaust from passenger and employee automobiles, evaporative emissions from refueling aircraft, emissions from boilers, heaters and generators, and solvents from maintenance operations such as degreasing and coating."[61]

At Santa Monica, similar risk was also found:
"For carcinogenic risk, results of the assessment revealed that cancer risks for the maximum exposed individual who resides in proximity of the airport were twenty-two, twenty-six and thirteen in one million for the baseline, increased turbojet and piston operational scenarios, respectively. These values represent discrete cancer risks associated with airport related exposures. No background or ambient concentrations were incorporated into the risk exposures. No background or ambient concentrations were incorporated into the risk quantification. In consideration of the Federal Clean Air Act, emissions associated with airport operations were clearly found to exceed the "acceptable risk criterion" of one in a million.

Nevertheless, it is important to note that during the preparation of this assessment, several informational sources

---

[7] FEIR is an acronym for Final Environmental Impact Report

were found to be rather restricted offering limited data to perform the assessment and quantify community-based exposures. The most notable restriction was the limited availability of emission factor data and chemical species profiles for the aircraft source category. For example, although the US EPA has developed exhaust emission fractions to allow for the quantification of polynuclear aromatic hydrocarbons (PAH), data is unavailable to assist in the identification of discrete compound weight fractions emitted within the exhaust stream, as well as the necessary toxicological data (i.e., unit risk factors) to enable the quantification of risk. Notwithstanding, incorporation of these compounds would serve to enhance the assessment and increase community risk estimates."[62]

People do not know if it is a synergistic combination of chemicals that might be causing these illnesses, cancers and higher death rates, a few compounds, mutated compounds, some or little, over time or directly. Since people are exposed and usually develop cancer much later, it is very difficult to pinpoint one cause as the reason. It could be something from childhood, or many other factors including genetics, workplace and even individual predisposition.

One thing is for sure, statistics and evidence say there is a higher risk for people living near and working at an airport. These same people living closest to the airport have higher cancer and death rates. In my mind, this is enough evidence to necessitate action. We don't need more studies. It's been studied enough. While some are talking about what more should be done, people are getting sick and dying. People should be warned. They should be removed. The industry is enjoying the profits and benefits from their operations and can do more for people they might be harming but are ignoring this problem at the expense of people's lives. Shouldn't matter if there are enough studies or not. A few good ones already say it is dangerous. Get them out of there. Boeing Field has higher cancer, deaths and other illnesses significantly higher than normal similar to Sea-Tac within a corridor closest to the airport. The regulators cite other sources around Boeing Field, an option that doesn't exist for Sea-Tac communities. So for Sea-Tac they pinpoint lifestyle as a possible indicator. It's the airport.

The national brain tumor foundation has incidence of all types of brain cancer at 11.8 per 100,000 person population per year. Totals for SeaTac communities per year for all types of brain cancer, glioma and glioblastoma is 98 or 24.5 per year, more than double the national average for the five mile area. More than half of these are in the one mile area with far less than half the 100,000 person population. If I compare one third of the number with one third of the population then there should be 3.93 per year as an average but instead, there are 14, 350% higher than average. They said 1992 was an anomaly with higher numbers than all other years, yet tables in the 1999 work plan have higher numbers for many other years, particularly 1990 closely resembling 1992.

The community representatives' comments in written discussions with the SDOPH reflect the frustration they were experiencing with the process:

"December 1999 SeaTac Health report indicated that the number of breast cancer cases is lower than expected based on zip code data. This contrasts sharply with the Feb. 1999 SeaTac Health report Appendix A Table 3 census data; it indicated deaths from breast cancer are 33% higher for the SeaTac area than King County."

In August of 1998, the SDOPH work plan question 11 asked whether there are similar cases of brain cancer seen near other airports. By December 1999, the question had been dropped from the work plan.

In February 1999 as a conclusion to discovery, the analysis summarized some of their findings this way:

"Residents of the SeaTac Airport Community were at a higher risk for death from cancer and chronic obstructive pulmonary disease (primarily emphysema) compared to the King County population as a whole. Respiratory cancer, accounting for 30% of cancer deaths, was also higher in SeaTac. The excess in chronic disease deaths as compared to the entire county appears to occur in people younger than 65."[63]

Dr. Hulse who practiced family medicine in Highline at my invite once attended one of our CASE meetings and told our group he was seeing far too many young people living near the airport with cancer.

The report goes on to render some advice:

"The most important risk factors for chronic diseases include cigarette smoking, alcohol misuse, high blood pressure, obesity, physical inactivity, high blood cholesterol, and high fat/low fiber diet. All of these factors are associated with the leading causes of death in the SeaTac Airport Community including cancer, heart disease, diabetes, cerebrovascular disease, chronic ob-structive pulmonary disease, and cirrhosis.

Cigarette smoking is a major risk factor for heart disease, lung cancer, and many chronic and acute respiratory conditions. Alcohol misuse increases the risk of heart disease, high blood pressure, chronic liver disease, sexually transmitted disease, motor vehicle crashes and other unintentional injuries including falls.

In addition to lifestyle risk factors, exposure to environmental hazards such as air pollution, toxic chemicals, and radiation can also affect health status. Poor air quality, both indoor and outdoor, contributes substantially to illness and death from respiratory diseases including cancer, chronic ostructive pulmonary disease, and asthma. Timely access to and use of prenatal care in the first trimester of pregnancy may reduce the risk of infant death and infant health problems. Smoking during pregnancy is also associated with an increase in poor birth outcomes.

Wearing a seat belt in a motor vehicle or wearing a helmet while riding a bicycle or motorcycle can prevent injury in an accident or mitigate injury severity. Firearms contribute to deaths...[64]

How about "Get away from the stinking airport." No, it's our fault again, our diets, our alcoholic cigarette smoking lifestyles. Maybe if we just get out of our indoor air polluted houses and off our fat rear ends and jog in the toxic plume maybe we wouldn't have all those diseases. I find it hard to believe that a survey that began with such alarm that it made a top news story on the evening news could end with advice on prenatal care and wearing a seat belt.

Doug at Ecology had written a proposal to go forward with a discovery process for some of the compounds that had been targeted by SDOPH as potential contributors to the higher than average disease rates. The director of SDOPH apparently retired in the meanwhile and nothing further has been accomplished that I am aware of besides a metals sampling which found significantly higher than normal levels of nickel and cadmium.

I have talked to a number of people over the years about these disease rates and emission estimates and always seem to go back to the same three basic questions. Are there emissions estimated at rates to cause disease? Yes, documentation confirms this. Are these emissions when put to a risk analysis expected to cause disease? Yes, EPA confirmed higher cancer risk at Midway Airport, experts echoed these results at Oakland and Santa Monica. Are there illnesses present that confirm these results. Yes indeed, higher cancer rates, higher death rates, lower life expectancy, higher hospitalization rates, etc. The causal relationship and outcome is clear to me. Jet emissions are extremely dangerous and millions of citizens are being constantly exposed. Cancer death rates 10% higher around Sea-Tac applied to the nation's 50 busiest airports is equal to 10,000 people suffering and dying prematurely. Our worst natural and man-made national disasters pale in comparison. So my question is why have sympathetic administrators and agencies always backed down in the end? Who or what is forcing them to downplay, dispel and ignore originally alarming information? I often asked; where is that last rock I'm going to turn over to find the real bad guy behind all this?

Higher liver cancer rates that could be attributed to trichloroethylene found by MFG to be above the ASIL are related to alcohol abuse even though nothing points to higher alcohol consumption by residents. Significant lung cancers are blamed on smoking, even though no data on smokers for the Sea-Tac communities exists and there isn't enough science to figure out the brain tumor problem. Terrible alarming numbers of horrible cancer deaths are in the end dismissed as if they are a lifestyle problem.

Disillusioned by so much work producing so few results, I had to stand back and re-evaluate what I was doing. It seemed every avenue sure to bring about victory in our local battle had been exhausted. EPA, Army Corps, Ecology our congressman, now the SDOPH all dropped the ball on us. Why? The legal team was always the last bastion of hope for us so no matter how downtrodden we were. They were fired by the ACC and not replaced. With that possibility taken away, the agencies giving up, key people quitting, and a very tired group, I had to quit the fight, at least, for awhile.

Chapter 18

CHRIS

Even though I was no longer President of CASE, was no longer working for RCAA and had retired from the "cause", I still managed to attend a meeting or two, although I wasn't sure why.

At one of the meetings, candidates for Port Commission were introduced and a young man named Chris Cain spoke. We had heard his kind of talk before, he would make changes, be more accountable to the people, fix problems, oppose irresponsible projects like the third runway, etc. Oh, sure. They all said that.

By this time, I had become so skeptical, not just of people who say one thing and then do another, but of so many wrongs by so many agencies that it hardly seemed worthwhile to support anyone for any reason. Even if the candidate had the best intentions, they would be up against so much corruption they would either be stymied from doing anything, run out of office or eventually bought off.

I had always thought that if you were honest and did good things that you would eventually be rewarded or exonerated. I haven't changed my opinion about that, just my idea of what the time-line might be. In this fight though, dishonesty prevailed at every turn.

Chris didn't have a chance, but he wanted to meet with me to get an education on what had happened so far. I jokingly asked if he had a year. He said he had as long as it would take. I was impressed with his willingness to be bombarded with Airport 101 as I had been with Minnie so many years earlier. Maybe Chris would be the one who I could pass on the files to who could then pave the trail leading to victory.

The runway construction would take years and as long as it was not yet built, in my mind, there may still be some hope.

I continued to work with the national group, finding they were all doing the same things on a bigger scale as the small group had done. There were 24 groups now as members of US-CAW representing communities all over the country, but each respective group, although having a hundred or more members, some even 1,000, had only a few active people. The group leaders were so involved with their own local efforts, there was little time for the national endeavors and each of us had a different agenda we wanted to push to the forefront.

We all agreed however, to write collectively to President Clinton and Vice-President Al Gore appealing to their environmental platform. We had heard that Vice President Gore was advocating legislation to protect natural quiet in national parks. For instance, small planes flying over the Grand Canyon were interfering with visitors' enjoyment of natural quiet as they observed the cliffs. Even though we thought it was ludicrous they were more concerned about park noise disturbing a dozen people 3 times a day and not at all concerned about jet noise disturbing one million people 1,000 times each day, we still held out hope they might also show concern for this collective CAW group pollution problem.

Their response included the usual, thanks for writing to us, and we will keep your thoughts in mind as we press forward toward fiscal responsibility. I have found that every politician who has said they are for the environment has been as unresponsive to us as the ones typically pro business on the other side.

Somewhere along the way, Jack, Frans, Steve and I began a discussion about way-ports. I understand Jack's position, living near the busiest airport in the country, O'Hare. He wanted flights moved to another brand new airport in Peotone. Who could blame him?

What Steve maintained is that if an airport were built in Peotone, it probably would be a reliever, not a replacement. Knowing how terrible it is to live by an airport and how hard we fight to educate everyone on the disproportionate and unfair burden of health problems we are bearing for the convenience of a few flights and travelers, how in the world could we advocate building more of the same and subjecting some new set of victims to the kind of nightmare we live?

This supplemental airport scam is the same thing that was used in Australia with Badgery's Creek. Every time the neighbors near KSA got boisterous about the impacts and inequities involved with the proposed expansion of KSA, the government would start to discuss a new airport at Badgery's Creek. Just like the discussion at Sea-Tac of putting operations at Paine Field and presently with building a new airport, these are tactics meant to sidetrack that probably have no real intention behind it except to cause delay and disorientation among the opposition.

Frans could not agree to the way-port idea because his philosophy of sustainability focuses on providing alternatives to jet travel, using jets only when absolutely necessary and other modes such as rail, to replace short hops. He couldn't support a new or reliever airport at Peotone over efficient and sustainable rail alternatives. All of us agreed we had decided in the very beginning we were not going to get involved with local battles.

At first, I told Jack that US-CAW might support the way-port idea but after talking to Steve and Frans I realized that was not possible. We can't logically advocate building more airports anywhere. Would the communities suddenly affected by a new airport become members of the national group who politically advocated the advancement of their suffering?

Jack took it pretty hard. This disagreement caused Jack to leave the national organization and Frans took up the presidency with Steve and I remaining on the board. I learned a lot from Jack and we had some good times working together. But we did not accomplished many of the things we set out to do. I do think though, that some little cracks we might have started will someday turn into busting dams, but we'll see. I don't think any progress has been made toward a new airport at Peotone save for a few blurbs in the news. Presently US-CAW agreed (with Steve dissenting and withdrawing and me whining and complaining) to put together a proposal for the study of a national transportation system which would include integrating air travel and way-port construction with rail and bus links as an intermodal unit which is the norm for some areas in Europe.

Recently, an air transportation committee in the Northwest, after two years of meetings and deliberations about future needs for the region, decided to do nothing. Apparently the FAA's wild forecasts have fizzled out twice since the EIS. It took several years for Sea-Tac to work its way back up to 1998 levels after 9/11 and again during the recent economic slowdown we are back down to pre-1994 levels. After predicting they needed the third runway to accommodate up to 500,000 operations by as early as 2010, they had only 350,000 last year (2009). The committee decided that Sea-Tac has enough capacity (they haven't called it fog relief since the SEIS) to last to 2030.

RCAA and CASE occasionally mention relief can be realized with more commercial service at Paine Field. Many have advocated spreading the problem around the region. I am not opposed to sharing the burden, but I am opposed to being part of the cog in the wheel that pushes it on other helpless victims. I asked Paine Field residents who must be living in fear from time to time to join with me to find a way to limit the power of the FAA, the real enemy.

As long as communities fight each other, little progress can be made. Sometimes it can have devastating effects. Steve had befriended a man, Richard, who lived right under a brand new flight path that was created as a result of local community and legislative pressure put on the New Jersey, New York routes. Richard was recording flights, noise levels and altitude of aircraft as they passed over his home. He was unable to sleep and eventually lost his job. Richard told Steve that he had tried to get help from the local activist group, but it turned out they were the ones who had put on the pressure in the first place to change the flight paths putting flights over his house. Richard met with Steve and was desperate. He couldn't sell his home, couldn't continue to make the payments without his job, couldn't get a new job in his condition of sleep deprivation, and didn't have anywhere to go. Steve was very troubled and concerned about him, but also did not have much to offer. Not too long after their meeting Richard committed suicide.

At one point Steve had left his house to stay in a hotel for a couple of days and found himself awake one night in a full sweat feeling he was in the grips of a post-traumatic stress experience. He had to move. Bill in New York had to take a $10,000 loss on his original purchase price to get out of his house in Rockaway. Bill depended on sleeping pills and couldn't take it anymore. Not too long after his move, a plane crashed into Rockaway neighborhood due to a mechanical failure.

Steve wanted revenge. Bill wanted sleep. Richard needed help. So many want relief, but still, nobody is listening.

Chris did not win a seat on the Port Commission, but he got a large percentage of the vote and ran a good grassroots campaign against an incumbent who spent tens of thousands more than he did. He ran again two years later and I agreed to be his treasurer. Again, he was defeated but not by many votes. Chris aligned himself with other disgruntled victims of Port operations, including waterfront fishermen, Georgetown residents and eastside developers to name a few. He decided to start a newspaper he called "The Port Observer."

He published his paper every quarter, depending on funds, and ran articles about Port operations and the downside of being on the bottom side of the Port's foot. He asked me to be a regular contributor so on occasion, time permitting, I would write an article about emissions and other issues related to our battle.

Chris continued to pick up documents from me. He would read a few, return them and get more. He was becoming pretty popular in the local CASE group too.

After my 7 year break in the action, Chris managed to convince me to look into greenhouse gas emissions from Sea-Tac. The Port had converted some of their taxi fleet to compressed natural gas (CNG) and in the wake of the big push on greenhouse gas emissions had released a green airport report along with a greenhouse gas emission estimate.

Many European reports have been published about the greenhouse gas issue and many point to aviation as a sector which has been ignored in the planning and protocol, a sector they claim is the fastest growing and single greatest contributor besides roadway vehicles. I have references to some of these in the appendix.

Again, as with many other things of the past, the Port has proclaimed itself a national leader in all they have done to help the environment, according to their "going green" report. Nobody really knows how bad they have made it, so anything they do looks great to the media, the public and special interest groups.

Chris talked me into going to a meeting with the Port Commission President, John Creighton. Chris and I met with him and another commissioner, Lloyd Hara. I made my presentation, brought all my mothballed documents, about a one foot tall stack, much of which I had pulled out of the archives for my recent meetings with a reporter writing an article about the GHG report. I discussed the emission load and the serious effects jet operations can have on human health and the environment. John seemed to be interested. But he had a concern. He was taking this information seriously and wanted to know if any other US cities or European countries have implemented emission controls of any kind. I knew that one European airport charged higher landing fees for planes with greater noise and emissions. Integration of different modes of transportation as an organized unit is also used in Europe. John expressed some hesitation at trying things that may not have been tried elsewhere. He wanted the same thing I wanted, a group of people saying and doing the same things to use as justification for bold ventures. It is difficult to make changes in an industry that modern academia or business has yet to even acknowledge as a problem and I understand John's hesitation. Even more difficult when there are only a few people even talking about the problems. I encouraged him to be a pioneer, someone people would look at as a hero years from now.

I never expect to hear anything more after a presentation like this. But within a couple of weeks, John had sent an e-mail message to the environmental staff at the airport asking intelligent emission related questions. He had managed in this short amount of time to become very knowledgeable. He must be a genius.

Chris suggested I make a presentation to the Port Commission centered around the greenhouse gas emission inventory and John said he would keep me posted on a date and time.

Even if the current popular global warming debate fizzles, there have to be long term consequences for spreading fossil fuel combustion by-products into the atmosphere at 30,000 feet. Maybe a far greater consequence than what we now realize. Spreading emissions into the upper atmosphere, according to some scientists, has twice the global warming effect than ground level because the emissions linger. Maybe it is because there are no trees or lungs up there to absorb it. These emissions also tend to be responsible for cloud formation. With the recent closure of many European airports due to volcanic eruptions, people saw the skies were a brilliant blue, something they had not seen for some time through the haze of emissions, apparently due to jet contrails.

If global warming issues prove to be as bad as some say it is, we may be causing irreversible damage that won't be readily apparent for decades to come. Then what? As I have said before and believe is true, there is no harm in cutting emissions, no harm in using airline travel responsibly, carefully and rarely. People somehow survived for millennia without it. I am not saying get rid of it. Just don't send half full jets 300 miles 20 times a day to the same destination. Especially when the least polluting per passenger mile high speed rail can get people there in less time.

A city planner in Boston recently told me there are occupied residences at the end of a runway near Boston Logan. That is ridiculous. And there are illnesses there! Neighborhoods and schools are located within three blocks of Sea-Tac boundaries on three sides. That is totally unacceptable. Since airports and FAA cannot afford to move the people away, the airport must be moved or its use changed. I advocate both.

My solution is radical. I believe these urban airports should be converted back to general aviation and light aircraft destinations with a jet airport built and buffered on at least 64,000 open acres far away from communities. The only problem with a jet based hub is they have to be built far away from sensitive land uses, preferably in the middle of nowhere. I also realize that when I advance this idea I am a hypocrite taking an opposite tact from my original view that no new airports should be built. Steve reminds me, there is just no middle of nowhere anymore.

You would never expect the new airport at Denver, buffered by 64,000 acres, to have a group fighting against the noise but there is one. People living on hills around Denver were being exposed to higher levels of noise they claimed was due to lower air pressure where noise travels further before dissipating. Planes that struggle to climb in this low pressure pass close to hilltop communities. One woman claimed her grazing horses were being driven mad. This problem makes it even more difficult to advocate building new hub airports away from communities. All I know is the present situation cannot continue without major changes. I do know jet operations and neighborhoods are not compatible. Citizens should never be forced to give up their lives and health for commerce and travel.

Maybe emission scrubbers could be affixed to blast walls built at runway ends although these will not help the residents in flight paths who are being toxic crop dusted by burnt fuel particles dropped over their heads by approaching aircraft. Aren't there skilled technicians and universities full of people who can figure this out? I don't claim to have all the answers, and development of new technologies or whatever it takes to reduce aviation emission impact needs to be just around the corner but is probably decades away. Meanwhile, as we wait for new engine technology, fuel modifications or whatever other emission reduction programs to be implemented, people need to be removed.

Chapter 19

The runway opens
November 20, 2008

"Governor Chris Gregoire today helped celebrate the grand opening of the third runway at Seattle-Tacoma International Airport and applauded the Port of Seattle for constructing a more efficient airport to benefit both tourists and business.

'The third runway will allow inbound flights to land on time even in the worst of weather.' Gregoire said. 'That makes airline travel more efficient and Sea-Tac airport a far more reliable destination for the world's airlines. Reliable travel is vital to our economy.'[65]

Recently, however, amidst community outrage at the constant use of the runway, the Port issued these alarming statements:

"When the Federal Aviation Administration's (FAA) air traffic controllers anticipate arrival delays **during good weather**, they also will shift some arrivals onto the third runway and use it along with the easternmost runway for arrivals. Port of Seattle and FAA documents on the third runway project have language stating that it will be used in this manner. While the most important justification for the third runway was very clearly articulated as reducing weather-related delays, other secondary benefits of using the runway in all weather conditions were not greatly emphasized. In retrospect, it is apparent that the focus on weather-related arrival delays has resulted in the primary *justification* for the runway being interpreted as the only *use* for the runway. *(bolding added)*

The FAA is clear that it will not restrict the use of the third runway."[66]

This can be contrasted with their response to comments on the third runway articulated in their FSEIS in 1997:

"A third parallel runway is needed to reduce arrival delay incurred during poor weather conditions."[67]

There were no other statements in the EIS indicating shifting arrivals or constant use. The region, cities, agencies and the public were told the runway was to alleviate bad weather delay, period. If the Port and FAA would have said it was a multi-use, all purpose runway, the EPA would have required more of an existing to future scenario use analysis for air quality. In that scenario, as my tables of impacts showed when I commented on conformity, the runway could not have been approved by EPA.

So who is the biggest liar? It's hard to tell. Was it the Port, their consultant or the FAA? Do any of the regional planners and the former Governor Locke feel embarrassed they were misled? Or did they know all along?

I had a conversation about the FAA's stated purpose and need comparing an existing airport with an expanded airport using the same numbers of aircraft in both scenarios with one of the technical experts at EPA in Ann Arbor when I was researching fuel use and

GHG emissions. I had heard the name Bryan Manning mentioned more than once in the past in my conversations with Region X EPA and the EPA in DC. He is a well known technical expert on aircraft engine certification and emission data. I contacted him to get emission estimates for the A-380 because I believed some airports across the country, including Sea-Tac may have a plan to introduce them. Since the engines on this jet are the largest I expected the output of NOx might be enormous. In my calculations, it would take only 5 takeoffs of this single jet each day to put annual tons per year of NOx over 100.

I mentioned to Mr. Manning that these airport projects need to compare between a build and no-build that adds polluters rather than hiding their figures behind ambiguous infinite capacity. He agreed it has been an issue, but as soon as I mentioned that someone should file a lawsuit against the FAA for skewing capacity to gain a positive conformity determination he seemed to cool. I noticed too that an assistant answered my questions in subsequent e-mails copying Region X EPA who have been strangely unhelpful and sometimes curt toward me since Jim left. Mr. Manning eventually told me their office would no longer be able to help me with issues related to Sea-Tac although my questions were not site specific up to that point. Just one more instance of people being helpful and interested at the outset only to completely withdraw when touchy issues come up.

The Port Commission

Sustainable Cascadia conference came to Seattle and Chris thought it would be a good idea to invite Dr. Frans Verhaagen from New York to make a presentation on his Ten Sustainable Aviation Demands. I am including those in the appendix to this book. Dr. Verhaagen has been the head of US-CAW for many years and has an extensive background in sustainability, teaching courses on this subject at various NY institutions.

Dr. Verhaagen did provide meaningful input at the meetings and was able to impress the Port Commission president, John Creighton with his expertise.

As an adjunct to the conference, I further made a presentation to the Port Commission in January 2008 and am also including the summary in the appendix as well. In November, 2008, SeaTac released an emission estimate of greenhouse gas (GHG) using the total amount of fuel pumped, nearly 2 million gallons per day, at Sea-Tac. The findings were surprising to some, nearly ¼ of the county total of Greenhouse Gas emissions (GHG) can be directly attributed to jets at Sea-Tac. This would mean that clearly, Sea-Tac is the largest single site source of GHG emissions in the county and most likely in the state, since King County has the state's highest overall emission totals. Nitrogen oxides, also considered a GHG were not included in the inventory which would have greatly magnified the results.

As a result of that presentation, the Port Commission voted to support our state joining the action sponsored by Attorney General Brown of California requesting EPA get involved in controlling airport emissions. Our state governor Gregoire, although pressing for GHG inventories, controls and standards, and our state AG both disregarded this recommendation when I wrote and asked for their support even though a number of other states had signed on.

A reduction strategy for one of the largest GHG producers in the state should be in the works, but I haven't seen anything targeting aviation. If included it must provide the polluter pay all. Anything less is unfair to other business, the general public and to the intent of any program which is reduction. Sea-Tac can easily buy offsets or credits from a smaller producer made affordable with their taxing authority and vast financial resources. This translates into us paying for them again.

I often wonder why GHG is suddenly such a popular item, while saving people from cancer causing emissions near large industrial polluters like airports never was. I don't know how harmful GHG is for the environment as a whole. I am aware of the debate back and forth and I am not a scientist so I am reluctant to take a position. My biggest concern about GHG is not so much the global warming effect still being debated, but all the cancer causing chemicals in the fuel that is a certainty. Cutting use of fossil fuels isn't going to hurt anybody.

Commissioner John has recently been involved locally with the first ever US commercial testing of bio-fuels. He told me airport tenants are using a new approach and direct- route flight patterns to save fuel and reduce emissions as well. Of course these things have a tendency to benefit the airlines because less fuel use is money saved unless bio-fuels are more expensive, who knows, at least they're renewable. That is critical.

While we are waiting for real solutions, each person can make a difference for our sustainable future. Since aviation is the most polluting per passenger mile of any other form of transportation mode, choosing to drive or taking the train will cut emissions. Frans advocated being a locavore. This is someone who consumes locally, from local growers and companies. This puts money back into the local economy, reduces waste and the environmental impact from shipping. Shipping five day ground which sometimes uses rail rather than air transport to transfer packages is how I receive everything I buy off the internet.

Recently

While driving through the airport along the edge of the new runway embankment, where they have planted trees and beautified the wall with a nature relief, I have noticed that every tree with direct exposure to the airfield has died. It has only been two years since they were planted.

Highline High School used to be separated from the airport by a half mile and a forest they removed for the new runway. Thousands of kids are running track and playing football right next to the new runway and dead trees. Exercise pulls the dangerous particulate deep into the lungs. I worry that some of these kids are being turned into future victims. I once told the superintendent in a packed public meeting room he should shut down the district and bus the kids to Kent which seemed pretty kooky to a lot of people at the time. What can I say? I'm afraid for them.

At a CASE meeting I recently attended, a married couple told me their daughter died at 40 of a brain tumor. She lived and grew up in the danger zone. I ran into Carl at the store today whose wife died two years ago in 2008 of glioblastoma brain tumor. They lived in the one mile area around Sea-Tac for 20 years. I don't believe brain tumors have gone down or that glioblastomas in 1992 was an anomaly. It happened then, and nothing has changed, so it will happen again and again until something does change. I have called the State Department of Public Health for current brain tumor statistics. They haven't responded to me. Like reporters and even Gina Marie Lindsey, they probably believe if it is as bad as I say it is someone would be doing something about it.

A lawsuit has been filed on behalf of the residents in the new flight paths for the third runway. Many of the homeowners who live in the flight paths to the north of the airport were absolutely shocked at the blatant disregard the airport had for their word on limited use of the part-time, (predicted 20% of the time) weather related, arrival only runway. Obviously, these residents were unfamiliar with history where the Port says one thing then does another. The runway's constant use is not justifiable since operations are well below 2006 levels when there were two runways and one half of a percent delay. But many residents were never insulated, no program has yet been implemented to buy-out these neighbors, and they are experiencing relentless disruption of their daily (and nighttime) patterns of living. All that the airport can do or say is they meant they would use the new runway all the time, and the community misunderstood. That is completely false. They said it would be used part time and only in inclement weather and the community believed them (well some of the community). These people somehow found a large law firm to take their case.

Contained in the complaint is a request for relief and/or an injunction from noise, fumes and soot from operation of the third runway. I was actually surprised they put soot into the complaint. I contacted the firm and let the lead attorney know I had a lot of information on emissions, some on soot and that I would be more than happy to provide them with the information I had accumulated over the years. They wanted to meet with me. But after a lengthy trial put off three scheduled meeting dates, they stopped trying. I was standing outside one of their public meetings with the local community carrying my one foot tall stack of documents ready to hand it over. One of the attorneys I offered it to looked at it, then me and casually said; can you just catalogue that and send it to us in an e-mail. After nearly 17 years of volunteer work, I felt a little insulted. He didn't even ask me what was there. Don't they have paid staff who could do what they ordered up from me? The Port Commission, historically, the natural enemy of the Sea-Tac communities, gave me more consideration than this guy. At any rate, this book will have to suffice. If they want to copy and keep my reference documents, I have that in a box ready to go. It's now a two foot tall stack of paper which doesn't include the three foot tall SEIS documents. They'll have to rent a U-Haul and get those from RCAA.

I would have loved to write a happy ending for this book, where citizens finally get compensated for all their suffering, the Port admits they haven't been forthcoming with the facts and some Erin Brokovich type of person gets a nice office. Fact of the matter is, there isn't a happy ending, in fact there isn't an ending at all. It's still ongoing. Paul Fitzgerald in Australia had a similar dilemma. He had to find an end point, write it down and call it good. The activist groups around KSA were still fighting the authorities in

Sydney with an ongoing Senate investigation at the end of his book. Jack in Chicago is still trying to get help for residents near O'Hare, the busiest airport in the country. Frans in New York is still writing and lecturing on sustainability. CASE still holds monthly meetings. Activist Stuart Jenner is monitoring noise in the communities and finding the Port's noise map is too small. An acoustic expert recently pointed out the Port's noise monitoring doesn't include low frequency. Arlene has some new studies which found aircraft noise causes a spike in blood pressure, while car, truck, bus and train noise doesn't have the same ill effect. RCAA is still open and running a web site. The Port & FAA are conducting their historically useless FAR 150 meetings writing down ideas they will never implement. Citizens are still outraged and complaining to the authorities while shuffling in and out of meetings like sheep. And me, well, it's obvious I still haven't quit, not really, not yet. As long as planes continue to fly over my head, I'll still fight it.

APPENDIX

THIS IS A SUMMARY OF A PRESENTATION MADE TO THE PORT OF SEATTLE COMMISSION AT ITS REGULAR MEETING ON JANUARY 22, 2008 AS A RESPONSE TO THE RELEASE OF INFORMATION ON THE CURRENT GREENHOUSE GAS (GHG) INVENTORY AT SEA-TAC AIRPORT

The Problem

- Aviation emissions (nitrogen oxides [NOx], which contributes to global warming) have increased by 133% in the period 1970 to 1998 compared to 3% or less for all other industry, which includes vehicles.[8]

- Aviation is the most polluting form of transportation per passenger mile of any form in the world while rail is the least.

---

[8] Controlling Airport-Related Air Pollution June 2003 NESCAUM, table, page I-7

- Aviation is the fastest growing source of climate changing emission in the European Union.[9]

- Aviation has by far the greatest climate impact of any transport mode.[10]

- By 2050, (Friends of the Earth [FOE] Europe predicts) aviation emissions will account for 40% of total <u>allowed</u> GHG emissions in an optimistic scenario and 50% by 2036 in the most pessimistic scenario.[11] *(emphasis added)*

- Emissions produced by the aviation industry is the only industry not regulated, controlled or monitored by the US EPA or state emission control agencies.

- Between 1990 and 2003 greenhouse gas emission from British industry fell in line with (the) Kyoto target. But as the Office of National Statistics has pointed out to the embarrassment of government Ministers, in this period greenhouse gas emissions from air transport rose by over 85%. (British Office of National Statistics July 22, 2004)

- Each enplaned passenger contributes four times their individual weight to Green House Gas emissions (approximately 300 kilograms).

- It is estimated that by 2050, in consideration that all other CO2 (carbon dioxide) sources will have continued to reduce emissions at present rates, forecast of aviation operational increases even allowing for improvements

---

[9] Aviation in a Low Carbon EU FOE Europe Summary Report 2006
[10] Clearing the Air The Myth and Reality of Aviation and Climate Change, T&E 06/2 CAN Europe 2006 ES page 4
[11] Ibid, statistic taken from Tyndall Centre on Climate Change, 2005

in aviation fuel efficiency, is predicted to be responsible for 1/4 total world global warming.

- Between 1990 and 2000 worldwide aviation emissions grew by 50% (Both above taken from "Fly now, grieve later", Aviation Environment Federation, Brendon Sewill June 2005 page 10)

- According to NRDC, "airplanes produced 350 million pounds of...VOC's (volatile organic compounds) and NOx (ozone precursors)...in 1993, more than twice their 1970 total. According to the US EPA, newer aircraft engines (are expected to produce) higher emissions of NOx. Most of the targeted goals for greenhouse gas (GHG) reductions such as the Emissions Trading Scheme (ETS) proposed by the European Union (EU) has not even included NOx from the aviation sector even though it is a known significant contributor to global warming

- 50 of the Nation's largest airports have undergone either expansion programs or planning for expansion in the last 10 years and operations are expected to double and even triple within the next 20 to 30 years

- Aviation landings and takeoffs spread emissions expected to have a ground level impact over many square miles outside the airport boundary.

- Past estimates of emissions have overstated surface transportation and airport ground support vehicles while understating emission impacts from jet aircraft. (see article at Port Observer web site: http://portobserver. com. Application of programs such as converting some vehicles to compressed natural gas (CNG), although notable, ignores the ever-increasing aviation sector and takes the emphasis off the real problem. The proposed ETS will not be effective unless the data is accurate and all emissions are considered, not just the landing-takeoff cycle (LTO)

- For the amount of fuel consumed by aircraft alone at Sea-Tac in 2006, 4.3 million metric tons of carbon dioxide was produced, 22% of King County totals.

Some Solutions

Even the FAA administrator has recently admitted that cutting flights is a reasonable step toward relieving congestion at the nation's airports, a concept seemingly never before thought of by the airlines and growth hungry FAA of the past. No amount of emission credit trading can accomplish what a flight cap or reduction can if any real reduction in the significant impact of emission totals presently produced by jet operations is desired. Friends of the Earth (FOE) Europe believes that at the predicted rate of growth, aviation may account for 100% of emission credit consumption by 2050 in an optimistic scenario leaving no credit left for any other industry. See:
http://www.foe.co.uk/campaigns/transport/news/aviation_ets.html

a) Fill the planes: Airlines are considering consolidation due to the current cost of fuel. Will help make aviation somewhat more sustainable, see ("Ten Demands" attachment)
b) Peak hour pricing: Transportation administrator has recently announced peak hour pricing as option, see: http://www.dot.gov/affairs/dot0508.htm http://blogs.usatoday.com/oped/2008/01/our-view-on-con.html
c) Emission cap: Allowing only the lowest emission jets to arrive and depart Sea-Tac while others pay an emission tax per pound above the cap

d) High speed rail as alternative: Least polluting mode per passenger mile

Higher Ticket Price

The idea of a cheap seat is not practical. The right price for air travel dictates that each passenger should pay a fare that reflects the actual cost of doing business, not subsidized business or business which ignores the real environmental effects.

a) **Internalizing environmental costs**: This would bring ticket prices up dramatically and effectively reduce demand. If airlines were charging $500.00 per ticket for all seats now sold at $100.00, especially for short hops to Portland, Vancouver BC and Spokane, destinations all accessible by car or even train, trips that are nearly as energy intensive as long haul flights, the resulting revenue could fund our state's portion of the **The Integraged Intermodal Transportation System** IITS, (see attachment)

b) Maintain the industry: Higher ticket price would help the industry pay its way and wean it off tax breaks and subsidies that other industry does not enjoy

c) Pay for past damage: Environmental clean up could create jobs. The resulting revenue stream will provide an economic benefit and funding for IITS

Taxing air travel

a) Taxing aviation: Using the same way passenger cars, fuel, property, loans and products are taxed is one solution that will decrease demand. See the report, "Fly Now Grieve Later": at http://www.aef.org.uk/downloads/FlyNowFull.pdf

Proper reporting

a) Must begin discussion with accurate and reliable information all parties can trust and verify.

b) Must be monitored by an independent agency such as EPA to guarantee accurate data distribution

c) Regulation:There is a need for EPA to regulate aviation emissions at airports. States need to sign onto California Attorney General Brown's proposal

The majority of the sources of CO2 **according to the recently completed Department of Ecology statewide inventory is automobiles with aviation and diesel vehicles combined as the second largest producer.**

Other Considerations

Department of Ecology's current Greenhouse Gas Inventory estimates statewide aviation GHG at 7.8 million metric tons per year (m/t/y) with diesel on road vehicles at 7.5 m/t/y in 2005. The total of these two is the largest category of GHG besides <u>all</u> automobiles and both are predicted to rise through 2020 while rail is constant at 0.8 m/t/y. Sea-Tac Airport 2006 figure of 4.3 million M/T/Y GHG is more than half the entire state aviation total.

Common predictions are for aviation operations to double or even triple in the next 20 to 30 years and this is the reason so many airports are engaged in expansion programs worldwide. However, the predicted future totals for aviation in Ecology's report do not reflect <u>that</u> forecast unless they foresee some kind of dramatic measure in efficiency or GHG reduction, a prediction not supported by past practices or future goals according to European Federation for Transport and Environment. See report at: <u>http://www.transportenvironment.org/docs/Publications/2006/2006-06 aviation clearing the air myths reality.pdf</u>

The total GHG for rail in our state report makes it the least polluting form for passenger and freight mobility into the future. By using rail rather than semi-trucks to transfer goods, the freeways will be partially unclogged without any downturn in economic benefit to the region and transferring passenger traffic within the BC to Portland zone by building high speed rail can eliminate much demand on aviation while dramatically reducing GHG.

Emission Credit Trading or Auction (ETS): Using public/property tax dollars to buy emission credits or auction or trading carbon credits in the future by imposing a new tax that is externalized to some other sector other than the aviation sector, revenue that <u>can be</u> garnered from Port operations, will not force any change in efficiency, technology or environmental stewardship. As the need goes up, the tax can go up. Emission credit purchase by aviation is predicted to be at 100% by 2050 in the European Union which will leave no offset credit for any other industry if aviation continues to grow at current and predicted future levels. For more information on some of the potential problems with the ETS proposal, see report at: http://www.foe.co.uk/campaigns/transport/news/aviation_ets.html

Should Sea-Tac decide it only wants to be concerned about the Landing/Takeoff Cycle (L/T/O) of the GHG from fuel use at the airport, this will leave the majority and the most damaging of the GHG emissions in the upper atmosphere unaccounted for. Each airport must remain responsible for the inventory of GHG produced from the entire fuel pumped and not be exempted because they claim it is out of their control at some point in the L/T/O. No other industry has that advantage. Additionally, if we count only what is used within a certain area, such as the 5 mile corridor, we discount what is arriving and airports take responsibility for only a fraction of their entire contribution to GHG in this scenario.

Cheap Flights: The current idea that anyone who may ever want to fly should be able to do so is not practical. As stated earlier, cheap seats are not a reality. These are subsidized seats that are being paid for by the welfare of the federal government and the taxpayer at the expense of the environment and public health. Very little comes from the individual user and very little of the wealth being obtained by the airline industry is coming back into the communities taking the brunt of this environmental brute. All other industry is regulated and controlled and must clean up after itself. Not aviation.

Additional Links:

'Aviation in a low carbon EU' research by Tyndall centre at University of Manchester on how the EU Emissions Trading Scheme needs to be improved if aviation is to be part of a low carbon EU
http://www.foe.co.uk/campaigns/transport/news/aviation_ets.html

'Growth Scenarios' published by us in 2005, 1st work by Tyndall that shows how UK and EU climate targets are unachievable if aviation growth continues and with no increase in rate of technology improvement
http://www.foe.co.uk/campaigns/transport/news/tyndall_launch.
html

'Predict and decide' by ECI at Oxford University 2006, excellent and detailed look at the issue http://www.eci.ox.ac.uk/research/energy/downloads/predictanddecide.pdf

A major study to suggest is the NESCAUM study, commissioned by 8 Northeastern states and overseen by the USEPA:
http://areco.org/NESCAUM%20report%206.03.pdf

Debi Wagner
US Citizens Aviation Watch, Inc

TEN SUSTAINABLE AVIATION DEMANDS

The following *US Ten Sustainable Aviation Demands* were inspired by the citizen sustainable aviation movement in Britain in their response to their Government's 2003 White Paper on Aviation of December 2003:

#1. Rein back the unsustainable expansion of the National Airspace Redesign (NAR) Program
Being sold as an efficiency and safety program, the NAR program is expansionistic and will reinforce the unbalanced US transportation system in favor of the premium, i.e. expensive mode of air travel. Citizens have to push for the Fifth Alternative, i.e. Doing More with Less, for demand is often a function of capacity. Like the rationing of the limited capacity of the radio spectrum, rationing can be suggested as an approach to limited and reduced air space and airport capacity.

#2. Plan for a US integrated intermodal transportation system (IITS) where preference is given to the less energy intensive and less polluting surface modes of transportation
Citizen Aviation Watch, USA, Inc. is proposing the IITS Initiative, a supplemental $300 billion, 15 year program that would integrate air transportation with an efficient intermodal surface transportation system that includes an expanded and efficient rail system (mostly for freight), a national modern coach network, Maglev, etc. Short-haul air flights would be replaced by fast, not necessarily, high speed trains or maglev.

#3. Include air transportation emissions into any global warming legislation, programs and projects on an equal basis with other industries
No serious headway in reducing global warming gases can be made without reducing the aviation industry's emissions as is made clear in George Monbiot's recent book *Heat. How to Stop the Planet From Burning.*

#4. Recognize the limits rising oil prices will put on demand for air travel as we head towards $100 per barrel in a world where oil production has peaked or will peak soon
Given that air transportation is 4-10 times more energy intensive, high oil prices will inordinately affect the aviation industry

#5. Remove the tax give-aways the aviation industry enjoys
A complete overhaul of subsidies in all forms will push transportation planners towards integrating the premium mode of air travel with the less energy intensive and therefore less polluting modes of surface transportation, which may not be necessarily less expensive.

#6. Reassess air freight which currently pays no special tax as passengers do
Consider not only taxing air freight, but also reducing the amount of air freight by creating opportunities for people and industries to primarily use local resources.

#7. Reduce both the day and night time noise suffered by local communities, as well as the numbers of people affected
Though technically and operationally aircraft noise can be somewhat more reduced, the greatest reduction will come from a reduced number of planes in an integrated intermodal transportation system

#8. Respect the country's biodiversity and heritage, including ancient woodlands and listed buildings, if airports have to be expanded.

Healthy ecological and social systems are the foundation of quality of human life and of the larger community of life or Earth Community

#9. Revise the economic assessment of the aviation industry
In the interest of well-being of people and planet all industries are to be reassessed by the principles of ecological economics, so that they internalize both social and ecological costs of their operations.

#10. Rethink the "predict & provide" approach put forward by governments and the airframe manufacturers such as Boeing, Airbus, and Bombardier.
Influenced by the military-industrial complex's predict and provide modus operandi, the civil aviation industry is to reassess its link to the military and militarism.

For further information: Frans C. Verhagen, M. Div., M.I.A., Ph.D., environmental/sustainability sociologist, www.metronyaviation.org, www.us-caw.org; gaia1@rcn.com or 718-275-3932. Spring 2007.

INTEGRATED INTERMODAL TRANSPORTATION SYSTEM (IITS)

THE INTEGRATED INTERMODAL
TRANSPORTATION SYSTEM (IITS) INITIATIVE: A
Concept Proposal for a US Sustainable Transportation System in
the 21st Century

By

Frans C. Verhagen, M. Div., M.I.A., Ph.D., sustainability
sociologist,
Coordinator, IITS Initiative Steering Committee
President, SAVIA Associates International (SAI)
www.susavation.com;
President, www.metronyaviation.org and www.us-caw.org
Adjunct Associate Professor of Sustainable Aviation at www.
vaughn.edu , Sustainability Fellow, Green Institute, Washington,
D.C. www.greeninstitute.net
gaia1@rcn.com; 718-275 -3932; 917-617 6217
New York City
November 2007

INTRODUCTION

- The IITS Initiative is demand #2 in the TEN
  SUSTAINABLE AVIATION DEMANDS that the
  US citizen sustainable aviation movement has been
  presenting to the US Congress since spring 2007. These
  demands constitute a vision of a mostly activist network
  working towards an ecologically sustainable, equitable
  and accountable aviation industry
- The IITS Initiative entails a congressional authorization
  of $300 billion over a period of 15 years.

- A predecessor of IITS is the proposed Moynihan Visitors Center on Intermodalism which is a ten year effort to have the former TWA terminal (Saarinen Building) at JFK be reused as such. Most of the Visitor Center's steering committee members are also members of the present IITS Steering Committee.

RATIONALE

- Ecological necessity to reach targets in drastic GHG reductions in the face of the climate crisis by
  - o Reducing energy intensity in the transportation system where air transportation is 3-10 times more energy intensive than surface transportation
  - o Integrating and optimizing air and surface modes of transportation, thus satisfying the need for sustainability in aviation, surface transportation, and in mobility in general
  - o Stopping the expansion in the aviation industry based upon the finding of the incompatibility of an expanding aviation industry with the increased need to drastically reduce heat-trapping gases
  - o and emphasizing qualitative growth, i.e., the incompatibility of expanding the aviation industry with the increased need to drastically reduce heat-trapping gases
- Economic feasibility:
  - o creation of many excellent planning and construction jobs for all modes of air and surface transportation over a period of 15 years, leading to the US Sustainable Transportation Master Plan that would invigorate the US economy while protecting the wellbeing of the natural environment
- Political possibility:
  - o Increased public pressure for realistic global warming legislation which will include the aviation industry

o   The 2008 election cycle lends itself for raising the IITS Initiative profile

o   Nation-wide petition drive for ISATEA (Intermodal Surface and Air Transportation Efficiency Act) authorization bill in fall of 2009 where air funding is integrated with surface funding.

- International feasibility:

o   The EU is forcing the US to have its aviation industry included in global warming legislation while implementing its cap-and-trade system where pollution allowances will be auctioned off and not allocated free of charge

o   The countries in the Global South are imitating industrialized countries' transportation system, particularly adopting an aviation-centered transportation system instead of relying on river, road and rail systems, thus exacerbating the climate crisis problem for all.

CONTENTS

- Integrating air and surface transportation systems, thus complementing Moynihan's 1992 Intermodal Surface Transportation Act (ISTEA) and integrating AIR 21 and TEA 21, leading to integrated transportation funding and planning and the development of a US Sustainable Transportation Master Plan by 2025.
- Centering the new system around the less energy intensive surface modes of transportation by integrating air with rail, road, river and marine transportation systems, using forward looking studies such as Perl's Rethinking rail passenger, Monbiot's Rethinking freight—Monbiot and others
- Adjustment assistance to aviation industry to cope humanely with its reduced role in transportation, particularly in short-haul passenger and cargo flight; assistance in forming joint ventures with surface

transportation companies, thus transitioning from a single to a more diversified financial structure.

- An IITS inspired sustainable transportation system is being discussed and applied in the metro NY region and the Cascadia bioregion. Cf. www.washblog.com

STRATEGY

- Have the US citizen sustainable aviation movement, citizens, private and public transportation organizations sign on the ISATEA petition
- Generate publicity by both publishing domestically and internationally, by issuing press releases, by organizing regional conferences on sustainable aviation and the IITS Initiative.
- Applying for planning grants and/or funding venture

CONCLUSION

Without *vision*, people perish." Proverbs 28:19
"Whatever you can do or dream you can, do it. **Boldness** has genius, magic and power in it." Johann Goethe

TABLE OF ACRONYMS

ACC: Airport Communities Coalition, cities banded together to fight Sea-Tac expansion

AQ: Air quality

ASIL: Acceptable Source Impact Level, state limits on hydrocarbon emissions

ASNA: Airport Safety and Noise Abatement Act

BWI: Baltimore Washington International Airport

CAA: Clean Air Act

CASE: Citizens Against Sea-Tac Expansion, a grassroots community group

CO: Carbon monoxide

CO_2:   Carbon dioxide (commonly referred to as greenhouse gas)

DEIS: Draft Environmental Impact Statement

DNL: Day night noise level; standard industry noise measurement, a *yearly average*

ECOLOGY: Department of Ecology, state environmental protection agency

EDMS: Emissions and Dispersion Modeling System used by FAA to estimate aircraft pollution levels

EIS: Environmental Impact Statement

ESL: Environmental Systems Lab, California based company who was contracted to monitor emissions around Sea-Tac in 1973

EPA: Environmental Protection Agency, federal agency

EU:`   European Union

FAA: Federal Aviation Administration
FEIS: Final Environmental Impact Statement
FOE: Friends of the Earth (environmental organization)
FSEIS: Final Supplemental Environmental Impact Statement
FTBR: Federal Brain Tumor Registry of the United States
GHG: Greenhouse Gas
HOK: Hellmuth, Obata & Kassebaum, mitigation consultants
IWS: Industrial Wastewater Treatment System, the facility that treats wastewater at Sea-Tac airport
MFG: McCulley, Frick & Gilman, air quality monitoring team
NAAQS: National Ambient Air Quality Standards, for carbon monoxide, nitrogen dioxide, sulfur dioxide, ozone, particulates and lead
NEPA: National Environmental Policy Act
NO_2: Nitrogen dioxide
NO_x: Nitrogen oxides (includes nitrogen monoxide, dioxide, trioxide, etc.)
NRDC: Natural Resources Defense Council
NTBF: National Brain Tumor Foundation
PAH/PCH: Polycyclic aromatic hydrocarbons
PORT: Port of Seattle, owner and operator of Seattle Tacoma International Airport
POS: Same as above
PPM: Parts per million
PSRC: Puget Sound Regional Council, representatives for the four-county area planning transportation
PSCAA/PSAPCA: Puget Sound Clean Air Agency, formerly Puget Sound Air Pollution Control Agency, regional air pollution monitoring, reporting and control.
RCAA: Regional Commission on Airport Affairs, an umbrella organization
ROD: Record of Decision
SEIS: Supplemental Environmental Impact Statement
US-CAW: United States Citizens Aviation Watch Inc.
VOC: Volatile Organic Compound

REFERENCES

[1] AIR POLLUTION BY JET AIRCRAFT AT SEATTLE-TACOMA AIRPORT US Department of Commerce Environmental Science Services Administration Weather Bureau Technical Memorandum WR-58 Wallace R. Donaldson Salt Lake City, Utah October 1970 page 13 Figure 4

[2] Controlling Airport-Related Air Pollution NESCAUM, June 2003 page 1-7

[3] Washington State Greenhouse Gas Inventory and Reference Case Projections 1990-2020 State of Washington Department of Community, Trade and Economic Development/Washington State Department of Ecology *Center for Climate Strategies* December 2007 page ES-5 See also: http://your.kingcounty.gov/dnrp/measures/indicators/at-ghg-emissions.aspx King County GHG figure 2005 at 21.9 million metric tons total as ¼ of the state total with Sea-Tac contribution of 4.3 million metric tons per year.

[4] Emissions and Dispersion Modeling System 1994 version 9.l data for geomode 1, 4 DC-10, 747 respectively

[5] Port of Seattle Homeowner Handbook Revision 8/25/1994 page 44

[6] Ibid page 42

[7] Ibid page 42

[8] Ibid page 24

[5] Washington Research Council Special Report Washington's Public Ports June 30, 1990 page 9

[10] Ibid page 5

[11] Ibid page 8

[12] Ibid page 2

[13] Port of Seattle's use of tax money...Seattle PI 6/25/09

[14] Tax at a Glance HYPERLINK "http://www.portseattle.org/downloads.taxpdf Levy.doc" www.portseattle.org/downloads.taxpdf Levy.doc updated 12/30/08

[15] Port a big user of taxpayer subsidies Seattle No. 1 on continent, study contends Seattle Times South Edition December 30, 1994

[16] van **de Pol**, **(1998)** The Myths of Flying Putting **aviation's economic** benefits ...

[17] Air Pollution by Jet Aircraft at Seattle-Tacoma Airport" US Department of Commerce Environmental Science Services Administration Weather Bureau, Wallace R. Donaldson WR-58 October 1970 page 6

[18] Late Dr. Allan Greene VP of SAFE in NY source is not cited in the letter

[19] Highline Times DesMoines News Jennifer Steiner January 1992

[20] Seattle-Tacoma International Airport "Air Pollutant Contribution" Department of Ecology Air Quality Program, Olympia, Washington May 1991 page 23

[21] Ibid page 21

[22] Ibid page 22

[23] "A Guide to Commonly Encountered Toxics" 'Hazardous Chemicals Desk Reference, Richard J. Lewis Sr. 2nd Edition 1991 Van Nostrand Reinhold

[24] Frankfurter Allgemeine Zeitung January 20, 1988 translated by Barbara Lucas Chin

[25] Estimation and Evaluation of Cancer Risks Attributed to Air Pollution in Southwest Chicago, submitted to: EPA Region 5 Air and Radiation Division

[26] Ken Feith USEPA Senior Scientist quoted in the Chicago Sun-Times Wednesday September 9, 1996 page 3

[27] Final Report Air Quality Survey Seattle-Tacoma International Airport McCulley, Frick & Gilman, Inc. Job No. 9029 January 1995 page 41

[28] Draft EIS Air Pollutant Methodology page D-101

[29] Ibid page D-99

[30] C W. Spicer et al; Chemical Composition and Photochemical Reactivity of Exhaust from Aircraft Turbine Engines 1986

[31] Draft EIS Air Pollutant Methodology page D-95, 96

[32] Scoping comments letter to Gene Peters, Landrum and Brwn dated June 16, 1994

[33] "Sea-Tac to hail bigger cab" 'Taller roomier control tower planned by 2002'Chris Genna Journal Business Reporter 1995 page B3

[34] Draft Environmental Impact Statement Air Pollutant Methodology page D-67

[35] Inside EPA's Clean Air Report September 19, 1996 pages 11, 12

[36] Highline Times, Des Moines News article by John Kaiser 4/26/1991

[37] Occupational Factors Associated With Astrocytomas: A Case-Control Study Robert G. Olin MD PhD and et al, 1987 page 18

[38] Environmental Systems Laboratory, Sunnyvale CA (ESL-ET59) 28 June 1973 page 7-1

[39] Port of Seattle correspondence to Ms. Lori Wardian dated August 29, 1995

[40] ESL page 7-5

[41] E-mail correspondence, May 4 2009

[42] ESL page 6-21

[43] Controlling Airport-Related Air Pollution NESCAUM, June 2003 page 1-7

[44] Controlling Airport-Related Air Pollution NESCAUM, June 2003 page 1-7

[45] ESL page 7-1

[46] Ibid page 7-2

[47] Final Supplemental EIS Appendix B Attachment A Comments on Draft Conformity Response to Comment #5 Page A-3

[48] Sea-Tac Airport Master Plan Update Draft EIS chapter IV Human Health pages IV.7-7, 7

[49] Sea-Tac Mitigation Costs Study, Executive Summary H.O.K. et al, February 1997 page ES-4

[50] Ibid

[51] Mayor Tom Jones of Olmsted Falls, FAA Listening Session, Volume II Appendices, Cleveland Hopkins International Draft Environmental Impact Statement October 1999 10/21/1998

[52] Congressman Dennis J. Kucinich FAA Listening Session, Volume II Appendices, Cleveland Hopkins International Draft Environmental Impact Statement October 1999 10/21/1998

[53] ADDRESSING COMMUNITY HEALTH CONCERNS AROUND SEATAC AIRPORT March 2000 page 2 Washington State Department of Health Washington State Department of Ecology Puget Sound Clean Air Agency

[54] Letter from SDOPH director Juliet Van Eenwyk to Senator Julia Patterson dated May 8, 1998 page 2

[55] Literature Review on Risk Factors for Glioblastoma Multiforme, Seattle-King County Department of Public Health, Epidemiology, Planning and Evaluation Unit and Washington State Department of Health, Office of Environmental Health Assessment Services (document is not dated) page 5

[56] Central Brain Tumor Registry of the United States Year 2000 Standard Statistical Report Table 5 page 15

[57] Amicus Journal by Renee Skelton Summer 1996 page 32

[58] Eastern Residents' Health Examined, October 6, 1999 Birmingham News by David Knox (Note: Ms. Mary Hendking, the health department community resource representative cited diet and smoking as likely culprits of these double the incidence of cancer rates in this community)

[59] Clean Air Report via InsideEPA.com 4/11/02 Vol. 13, No. 8 CLEANAIR-13-8-11 Dawn Grodsky

[60] The Sydney airport Fisaco by Paul Fitzgerald page 97 references for all quotes page 229

[61] J. Phyllis Fox, Ph.D., Russell Resources, Inc., Comments for Oakland Airport (12-97)

[62] Santa Monica Municipal Airport "A Report on the Generation and Downwind Extent of emissions Generated from Aircraft and Ground Support Operations prepared for: Santa Monica Airport Working Group Los Angeles Unified School district environmental Health and Safety Branch June 1999 7.0 pages 34, 35

[63] Health Profile for the SeaTac Community Seattle King County Department of Public Health February 1999 page 11

[64] Ibid page 12, 13

[65] Governor's Communications Office, press release 11/20/2008

[66] Port of Seattle 'Air Mail' Spring 2009

[67] Final Supplemental EIS Apendix c-2 page c-2-5 1997

A view of the runway plateau in the distance from Sunnydale Elementary School, built in 1882